Professor Verna

Wright Answers

Your Questions

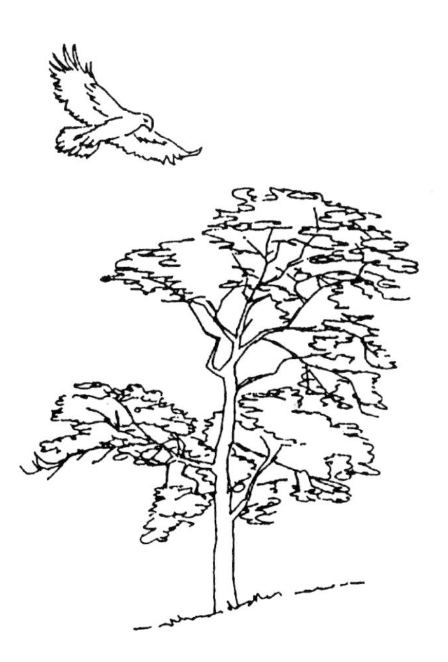

The questions and answers reproduced in this book were first published in Evangelism Today. *They appeared over a period of twenty years.*

Published September 1993.

ISBN 0 902548 39 5

Published by Day One Publications
6 Sherman Road, Bromley, Kent BR1 3JH

Designed and printed by Clifford Frost Ltd, England

CONTENTS

FOREWORD

A man with a view is at least worthy of a few minutes attention. A professor of medicine is not going to be an exception to this. Prof. Wright is more than a dry academic and 'Wright Answers' is much more than its title would lead you to think.

Collected here is the best of Verna Wright's answers to a host of questions from his regular column in the newspaper, *Evangelism Today*. They are the considered thoughts of a well read, carefully researched Christian leader who has constantly sought to live out what he believes. Like his Lord and Saviour, Verna Wright has often taken the rap for his uncompromising and biblical approach to life. He has not been blown by current, trendy winds of doctrine nor become rigid or bitter so that he lost contact with ordinary people. Verna is cherished, and in reading this book it will be evident why. I pray his views and principles will be as great a blessing to many others as they have been to me.

ROGER CARSWELL

THE BIBLE

QUESTION

Do you take every word of the Bible to be true and can you tolerate such religions practised by other communities of people?

ANSWER

Yes, I have every reason to believe that the Bible claim is true that 'all scripture is given by inspiration of God, and is profitable for doctrine, for reproof, for correction, for instruction in righteousness; that the man of God may be perfect, throughly furnished unto all good works' (2 Timothy 3 v 16,17). Some parts of the Bible are parabolic (eg the parables of Jesus), some are symbolic (eg the visions of Daniel and Revelation), some are metaphorical (eg 'you are the salt of the earth'), some indeed are the record of the devil's lies (eg in the garden of Eden) — but all scripture is a true record of what took place.

We should be tolerant of the adherents of other religions — the Crusades are a black spot on Christianity's history and the Inquisition even more so. At the same time we recognise the exclusive claims of Christianity — Jesus said 'I am the way, the truth, and the life, no man comes to the father but by me'. And again Peter declares in his sermon, 'There is no other name given under heaven among men, whereby we must be saved.' Other religions (Buddhism, Islam, Hinduism, Roman Catholicism, Jehovah's Witnesses, Mormonism, etc) teach we must do things to earn God's favour — New Testament Christianity is adamant that God has done all that is necessary for our salvation. So that in Christianity alone can one have the certainty of eternal life. Then again, Christ alone has risen from the dead.

QUESTION

Are the Gospel narratives of the resurrection contradictory? For instance, Matthew and Luke speak about the women seeing two angels, whereas Mark talks about a young man dressed in white.

ANSWER

This is well dealt with in John Wenham's book *Easter Enigma: Do the resurrection stories contradict one another?* The first and obvious thing is that the women were amazed at the sight of the 'young man dressed in white' — and that they were in awe of him. In other words he was an angelic being. Ultimately they 'fled from the tomb, for trembling and astonishment had come upon them — for they were afraid.' He was a supernatural young man.

As for the alleged discrepancy of one and two, that is nonsense. If there were two, there was one! In a scene when one person is the chief speaker or actor, it would be perfectly natural to omit reference to the irrelevant fact that he had a companion. We are dealing with two *descriptions* of an event and not with two witnesses replying to cross-examination. These witnesses are not answering the question 'How many?', they are giving incomplete descriptions of a complex event.

QUESTION

What should the Christian's practical attitude be to the written law of the Old Testament, especially now that he is under grace?

ANSWER

We have to be careful to distinguish between the ceremonial law and the moral law. 'Christ is the end of the law to everyone that believes.' The ceremonial law found its fulfilment in Christ. He was the last priest, who offered the last sacrifice (Himself) for sin. It is unfortunately true that the phrase 'under grace' can be an excuse for all sorts of behaviour. The fact that we are not under law brings us into the liberty of the sons of God and is not an excuse for licence. The apostle Paul says that 'Love is the fulfilling of the law.' The word 'fulfilling' carries the sense of 'fills in the loopholes'. So the fact that we are under grace (i.e. constrained by love) means that where we might try to evade the letter of the law we will now be concerned to keep it not only in letter but in spirit also. It is in this sense that Jesus sharpens the thrust of the commandment in the Sermon on the Mount, where He says that you do not need to commit an act of immorality to be an adulterer, but to look with lust suffices. Every Christian would wish to keep the Ten Commandments out of love to His Lord.

It should be stated also that we must preach the law to bring conviction of sin. The New Testament makes it plain that sin is the transgression of the law. This is particularly important to stress in an age when there are few objective standards and where we may be tempted to preach a Gospel which offers men an experience, rather than pardon from guilt.

CHRISTIAN LIVING

QUESTION

I am in a Christian Union where it is not uncommon for members to swear. What do you think of this?

ANSWER

1. Swearing usually demeans either God or sex.

2. When Peter wanted to deny His Master he laced his language with oaths and curses. You should feel therefore that to swear is to deny the pure Saviour whom you follow. I do.

3. Jesus clearly taught that our Yes should be Yes and our No should be No. If we are men and women of our word, then it will not be necessary to underline our statement, with swearing. That is the teaching of the Sermon on the Mount.

4. I rebuke swearing among academics, whose insecurity is sometimes manifested by bad language — so I certainly wouldn't condone it among professing Christians.

5. I appreciate that if you are constantly in an environment where swearing is the norm, a swear word may slip out. The Lord understands — come in repentance and the Saviour's blood will cleanse. Remember that on the cross, Jesus died for what Matthew Henry calls 'tongue sins'. Prophetically it was said of Jesus, 'My tongue cleaves to my gums.'

6. At Pentecost when the Holy Spirit was generally given, that experience was marked outwardly by tongues of fire, and inwardly by new tongues. So as far as an uncontrolled tongue which brings dishonour to God is concerned, we may say, 'These things *should not be.'* And by the power of the Holy Spirit we cry, *'These things shall not be.'*!

QUESTION

When there are so many demands on our lives, how do we choose our priorities and keep sane?

ANSWER

1. The New Testament certainly enjoins that we should be hard at it for the kingdom of God. Jesus gave His motive for being stretched to the limit 'for the night comes when no man can work'.

2. Jesus maintained balance by periods of prayer.

3. The promise is 'He gives power to the faint; and to them that have no might He increases strength'. The Lord is not looking for an able man but an enabled one. Moreover, 'they that wait upon the Lord shall renew their strength; they shall mount up with wings as eagles; they shall run and not be weary; and they shall walk and not faint' (Isaiah 40 v 29-31). From turmoil to tranquility there are two wings, prayer and praise.

4. Our motive and good must be ever before us. Remember, a fanatic is a man who re-doubles his effort when his aim is forgotten.

5. Recollect the dimensions in which work and labour are set in the New Testament. 'Your work of faith, and labour of love, and patience of hope in our Lord Jesus Christ, in the sight of God and our Father' (1 Thess. 1 v 3). To the church at Ephesus 'I know thy works, and thy labour, and thy patience' (Revelation 2 v 2).

6. When Carey was asked what attributes for service he had, he replied 'I can plod'. Taking a leaf out of his book, when folk ask how I fit everything in, I reply, 'I work'.

7. Our priority is to keep near to the Lord.That doesn't usually mean less work but more discipline. As a university student I was often amused by vigorous discussions about whether Christian Union members should do more academic work or more directly spiritual activity. As if there wasn't a third sizeable area to consider — wasted time!

QUESTION

How should a Christian differentiate between 'judge not' and 'judge all things' i.e. constructive and destructive criticism?

ANSWER

It is important to see these two statements in context. The first, 'judge not' prefaces the simile of the splinter and the beam in a person's eye (Matthew 7 v 1). It is warning us against adopting a critical attitude towards others when all the time there are far worse failings in our own lives which are unchecked. The second, 'judge all things' is found in 1 Corinthians 2 v 15 where Paul says 'he that is spiritual judges all things'. The word 'judge' is the same as that rendered 'discern' in the preceding verse, 'the natural man receives not the things of the Spirit of God, for they are foolishness unto him; neither can he know them, because they are spiritually discerned'. The Christian, because he is indwelt by the Spirit of God, has spiritual discernment not possessed by the unconverted man. We are certainly told to make right judgements, shunning sinful practices and false doctrine ('shun vain and profane babblings') and at times having nothing to do with evil men who pervert the truth and lead many astray.

QUESTION

Some Christians in the face of the most heinous crimes say: 'I forgive them'. Is this right?

ANSWER

It is important not to minimise the gravity of crime — especially those against persons. Here then are some general principles:

1. Crime must be punished for the sake of society, for the benefit of the person, and for the fulfilment of natural justice, which has been decreed by God.

2. The punishment should fit the crime.

3. Forgiveness can only be realised if it is requested and received. In the days of capital punishment the judge as he pronounced sentence would conclude 'May God have mercy on your soul.' Thus he commended the murderer to God's perfect judgement and justice, and if they repented, to His mercy. Repentance is a vital necessity for someone to be the recipient of God's mercy.

4. These strands of thought are brought together in Romans 12 v 17-13 v 4: 'Do not repay anyone evil for evil . . . Do not take revenge, my friends, but leave room for God's wrath, for it is written, 'It is mine to avenge; I will repay,' says the Lord. On the contrary: 'if your enemy is hungry, feed him; if he is thirsty, give him something to drink. In doing this, you will heap burning coals on his head.' Do not be overcome by evil, but overcome evil with good. Everyone must submit himself to the governing authorities, for there is no authority except that which God has established. The authorities that exist have been established by God. Consequently, he who rebels against the authority is rebelling against what God has instituted, and those who do so will bring judgement on themselves. For rulers hold no terror for those who do right, but for those who do wrong . . . If you do wrong, be afraid, for he does not bear the sword for nothing. He is God's servant, an agent of wrath to bring punishment on the wrongdoer.'

QUESTION

Is it right for a Christian to have a hobby? I was brought up with a company of godly and separate Christians who taught that God's people should be totally absorbed with Christ and heavenly things to the virtual exclusion of all worldly pursuits, including hobbies. In more recent years I have been tempted to take up a hobby (eg ornithology) but I feel guilty about this because of my childhood teaching. I would be glad of your advice about this.

ANSWER

In answering this question a number of points must be considered.

1. Separation is an important Biblical doctrine which is little taught in our churches today to their great detriment.

2. We need a careful definition of the world however. There is God's created order of things which was stamped on each day with the words 'it is good'. Matter is not evil. There is the world of people which God loves (John 3 v 16). Thirdly there is the world from which we are called to be separate — it is the system organised in enmity to God. It is well summarised in 1 John 2 v 15,16: 'Do not love the world or anything in the world. If anyone loves the world, the love of the Father is not in him. For everything in the world — the cravings of sinful man. the lust of his eyes and the boasting of what he has and does — comes not from the Father but from the world.'

3. 1 Timothy 4 v 4,5 clearly teaches, 'For everything God created is good, and nothing to be rejected if it is received with thanksgiving, because it is consecrated by the Word of God and prayer.' God has given us the natural things in this world to enjoy.

4. It would appear that David played the harp as a hobby — he wasn't a professional musician. God used that hobby to good effect.

5. It is a false distinction to believe that things are unspiritual if we are not consciously totally absorbed in Christ. To my secular work I have to be totally engrossed in it for periods — but I still do it 'as unto the Lord' (Colossians 3 v 23). Likewise the enjoyment of a hobby as it refreshes me may make me better fitted to serve the Lord.

6. A hobby becomes wrong when it is so absorbing that it supplants the Lord in my affections. If it holds me back from evangelism, if it stops me going to the prayer meeting, or if it diminishes my time of personal Bible study, then the hobby has assumed a place of undue importance. A friend of mine was a keen cricketer (Yorkshire standard, so you can tell he was really good!). He stopped playing when he said it became bail worship!

7. Speaking as a man who puts baskets of peanuts on the tree in front of my study window, so I can enjoy the bluetits feeding, and who scatters bread and fat meat on the concrete so I can watch the other birds, I hope you enjoy your ornithology — and if you discover how I can stop the squirrels stealing the nuts meant for the bluetits, would you let me know please?

QUESTION

How do you get out of a rut?

ANSWER

A rut is a hole you can't get out of in a place in which you do 'the same old things' and they lose their meaning because of repetition. It has a bad effect because it may put pressure on you, making you feel moody; it may stop you growing and it may stop you going forward in the work of God.

There are different sorts of rut. Young people often think they are in a rut, whereas it is the impatience of youth. Older people are often in a rut and don't realise it.

A Christian may at times feel he is in a rut because he sees little immediate fruits regarding the missionary working year after year in a Moslem country or the faithful Sunday School teacher. Doubtless the devil at times tries to make us *feel* useless. This calls for the grace of perseverance. We should ask ourselves, '*why* am I doing these activities?' Our attitude is all important. It is refreshing to remind ourselves of God's call in response to human need. We should also ask ourselves whether we can improve the way we are doing things.

On the other hand we may be in a rut which is thoroughly bad. The steps we should then take are:

1. Analyse the problem. Are there areas of our lives displeasing to the Lord, wrong television programmes being watched, wrong books being read, unseemly conversations in which we are joining? Are there areas of our life unsurrendered to the Lord?

2. Check up on your Quiet Time, and seek the Lord's will in prayer.

3. Get to grips with God's Word, the Bible, personally and in group study.

4. Talk the matter over with a Christian friend.

5. Especially seek the help of an older Christian friend — do not, however, deliberately go to one who will give you the answer you want to hear. Much less, go from one to another, until you find someone who will counsel you according to your desires.

6. Avail yourself to the fellowship and teaching of a good Bible-based house party. The Lord often speaks to us over a weekend or a week set apart with Him.

7. Don't sink into a morass of self-pity. Get stuck in and be active in the Lord's work. Too many people are waiting for God's green light to say go, whereas they should proceed with what is sensible until God flashes His red light to say stop. This was the attitude of the apostle Paul. He assayed to go into Bithynia (a sensible piece of outreach), but the Spirit redirected him.

QUESTION

I am a teenager — I don't have much to do in the evenings apart from Friday when there is a fellowship meeting, and Saturday when there is a prayer meeting, Bible study, and open-air meeting. Suggestions or advice, please?

ANSWER

This question was asked at a young people's house party. The answer is reproduced by kind permission of the Editor of the *Bedford Young Life Campaign Bulletin:*

1. As you have some of that seemingly unobtainable thing, spare time! What do you do with it? As with all difficulties, find out Scriptural principles which apply. Here are some for this case.

(a) I belong to the Lord absolutely — therefore this includes my time. (b) I am to mature and develop in character and personality into the kind of person God expects me to be; the things I do should have this aim (c) I should develop all and any skills which will make me a more useful Christian worker.

2. Let's be practical. Having prayed about it — (essential) — I find that I am a lazy person. So I will take steps to overcome it, at the same time learning a practical skill. What about cooking (or, for the fellows, doing some household maintenance?) Can't boil an egg? — ask Mum if you can help with dinner — this is the best way to learn. Or ask for a recipe book for Christmas — you'll be surprised how easy it is to follow instructions and make something good! Don't forget every beach team needs a good cook and somebody has to provide refreshments at certain evangelistic events.

3. Maybe laziness is not your special failing — but you lack discipline — or a sense of responsibility. Set yourself a task of learning Scripture — it CAN be single verses, but how much better to learn whole psalms or chapters. Keep at it and do it with others.

4. Or take on the responsibility of visiting. How about a REGULAR visit to an older person in your Church? Do his or her garden — or shopping — or posting.

5. Do you have the fault of starting things and not finishing them? If you are musical, see if you can purchase or borrow an accordion and a chorus book; you could soon be playing. 'He made the stars to shine' on Llandudno beach! Again, this is far better and more fun if two or three of you do it together.

6. If not musical, are you a bookworm? No? Well, that's another skill to learn. A good missionary biography is not hard to read, and even if it is, for you, keep at it, and you will not only gain knowledge from the book, you will develop your powers of 'stickability.' (This is a very valuable quality in the Christian life.) Many older Christians are only too glad to lend their books — try asking.

7. Decide where you are aiming and then make a PLAN. Develop kindness and thoughtfulness by what you do to others; there are always folk in the fellowship who are still lonely — (can you visit them? . . . do things together) — lots of parents who would appreciate not only a helping hand, but a demonstration of love and affection, by your thoughtful actions. Remember, you will not always have time on your hands. Don't one day have to look back and wish you had given your parents more of your love and care; or had learned Scripture and studied more while you had time and an active mind.

8. If you're still stuck, think about evening

classes . . . car maintenance . . .first aid . . . languages . . . Use your initiative. Develop it by PLANNING and DOING something . . . and carrying it through.

9. Work hard; pray hard; play hard; get Christian character and practical skills, in your available (not 'spare') time.

QUESTION

When it comes to spending money, how do you distinguish between necessities and luxuries? e.g. If you had a slightly shabby chair, would you consider it right to spend money on loose covers or is this an unnecessary extravagance?

ANSWER

In the final analysis this is an issue you must weigh up before the Lord. Cultural factors cannot be excluded — what is necessity to me in England may be luxury to the man in an underdeveloped country. I should not sit in judgement on a fellow Christian in this matter. Principles that may help you to decide the issues are:

1. I am a steward of God's gifts. The man who stole is to steal no more but work with his hands *that he may have the wherewithal to give to others.* However, it is not always the best stewardship to buy the cheapest. On a rare occasion when my wife unwisely allowed me to shop, a man sold me a cheap carpet saying 'it would wear clean.' It did — it wore clean through in no time! Chair covers may well prolong the life of furniture — good stewardship.

2. Shoddy appearances can be a poor witness. At the turn of the century you could tell those in slum streets who got converted — their houses became neat and tidy. As with clothes things should fit and be fitting. Social factors cannot be ignored in this context.

3. Money (and material possessions) are not to be stored but distributed. For a Christian, coins are made round to be rolled, not flat to be stacked. Perhaps that is a good argument for keeping your balance to coins, not notes!

4. Prosperity has great dangers. We have commented previously on the throttling effects of riches on our spiritual vitality. Houseproud owners who keep things so spick and span there is no welcome for thoughtless guests, receive no commendation from scripture. One favourable comment about Christians referred to in Hebrews was they took the spoiling of their goods joyfully.

5. Our tendency is always to go up in the world not down. This is in sharp contrast with the Lord Jesus, who emptied Himself. His life was one step down after another. The extent to which we will be a blessing to others is doubtless gauged by the extent to which we empty ourselves. It is a divine principle.

6. Our whole attitude to giving requires review. Our giving should be regular, systematic and proportional (1 Corinthians 16 v 2). But it should also be sacrificial. The challenging action of the widow who put her mites in the Lord's treasury earned the Lord's approval. Her giving could have gone not on luxury but on necessities. How this applies to us we must sort out prayerfully before the Lord.

QUESTION

Is it correct to enjoy non-Christian entertainment?

ANSWER

We have to distinguish between non-Christian and anti-Christian. Non-Christian activities may help or hinder depending on the context. For example, I've enjoyed immensely reading *The Diary of Anne Frank* — this moving document is not Christian; she was a courageous Jewish teenager in Holland who died in a Nazi concentration camp. The book gave me an insight into teenage thinking, as well as being thoroughly enjoyable. If it stopped me going to my church prayer meeting, it wouldn't have been helpful. Or again, my son beating me at table tennis was fine — unless it prompted me to cheat to beat him at least once! On the other hand books that debase or entertainment that stirs up wrong passions could be classed as anti-Christian. Some guidelines are therefore required.

1. Is it healthy?

   My body is the temple of the Holy Spirit and I am to glorify God in my body. Any entertainment which damages my physical health is wrong. My mind is to be under the control of the Holy Spirit. I am to be transformed by the renewing of my mind (Romans 12 v 2). Anything which corrupts my mind is to be abhorred.

2. Does it meet the criteria of Philippians 4 v 8?

   'Whatsoever things are true, whatsoever things are honest, whatsoever things are just, whatsoever things are pure, whatsoever things are of good report; if there be any virtue and if there be any praise, think on these things.'

3. Does it hinder me in my spiritual walk?
4. Does it hinder others in their spiritual walk?
5. Does it help me in my spiritual walk?
6. Does it help others in their spiritual walk?
7. Would it cause the Lord Jesus to say to me, 'Yet one thing is needful'?

QUESTION

What do you think about Christians watching soap operas?

ANSWER

Since I don't watch soap operas, I can answer the question dispassionately from basic principles.

1. Does the programme contain blasphemy? If so, don't watch it.

2. Does the programme contain swearing? If so, don't watch it.

3. Does the programme display divorce as the norm? If so, don't watch it.

4. Does the programme portray illicit relationships as exciting ones to be condoned? If so, don't watch it.

Should the soap opera pass these simple tests, then feel free to watch it if you have time.

QUESTION

What should be the Christian's attitude to sport?

ANSWER

As Joshua marched to Jericho he met a man with sword drawn. He exclaimed, 'Are you for us or against us?' This discriminating attitude must characterise our approach to everything — sport included. Certainly my colleague, Gerard Chrispin, who was associated with Yorkshire cricket found the Lord blessed him more by severing his connections with Yorkshire's team than by continuing — but this is an individual matter.
Principles to consider are:

1. Bodily exercise does profit a little. Most sports are good physically and from the point of view of relaxation.

2. Is Christ going to be first if I carry on?

3. If I carry on, and there is conflict with the call of Christ, will I be prepared to give it up?

4. Does it take up too much time and thought?

5. How does it accord with the principle of separation. The occasional game of tennis would certainly make out all right on this score. But how about professional football matches with their filth? And what about the clubhouse activities in rugby culture?

6. Am I able to hallow the Lord's day? Sunday sport is wrong. Years ago my friend, Hank Meeker of Baltimore, gave up a lucrative baseball career because games were played on Sundays. It has cost him dearly financially but the Lord has used him to head up a wonderful work at the Port Mission in that city.

7. Steps I take in relation to this may well be part of 'bearing the cross' and 'denying self'.

QUESTION

What comes first with a dedicated Christian, loyalty to his trade union or loyalty to his Christian faith? e.g. He may know that by withdrawing his labour from a public service he will cause untold misery to elderly people, young wives and children.

ANSWER

There can be no doubt that under any circumstances a Christian's loyalty is first to Christ. This is true in our relation to those in authority. As far as the state is concerned we should obey those that have the rule over us (1 Peter 2 v 13-14). Yet the same apostle who bade us to submit ourselves to every ordinance of man, when told not to preach the gospel publicly by the Sandhedrin replied that 'It is better to obey God than man (Acts 4 v 19). In other words, earthly authority is circumscribed and a higher principle prevails over certain areas.

That is not to say that strikes are always wrong. There has in the past been such a thing as capitalist exploitation and the trade unions came into being to enable the working man to obtain justice. The strike was one of his few weapons to achieve equality, and is recognised by the government of this country (although not of course by communist regimes!) as a lawful step.

I have every sympathy with your line of reasoning and feel the same about the medical profession. If your sense of Christian responsibility produces a conviction not to join a particular strike, then I would be guided by that. 'Seek first the kingdom of God and His righteousness' (Matt. 6 v 33).

QUESTION

How can young people defend themselves against the immorality and impurity of so much that goes on these days?

ANSWER

1. Be careful what you watch. Television, films, soap operas which inflame lust, depict impurity and take as normal standards that are far from biblical, will erode your defences.

2. Be careful what you hear. The same principles apply to radio plays as soap operas. The afternoon plays on BBC Radio 4, for instance, are usually appalling in moral terms. Avoid filthy conversations. Ephesians 5 v 3 and 4 are clear, 'But fornication and all uncleanness or covetousness, let it not even be named amongst you, as is fitting for saints; neither filthiness, nor foolish talking, nor coarse jesting, which are not fitting.' It continues in verse 12 'For it is shameful even to speak of those things which are done by them in secret.'

3. Positively, read books which edify and do not soil. 'Finally brethren, whatever things are true, whatever things are noble, whatever things are just, whatever things are pure, whatever things are lovely, whatever things are of good report, if there be any virtue, and if there is anything praiseworthy — medidate on these things.'

4. Link up with a group of out and out soulwinning young people. Their fellowship, activity and standards will help to make a bulwark against evil.

QUESTION

For 'A' Level French we have started to read a book which in certain parts is immoral. Faced with a similar situation recently, when the book was not for an examination, I made it clear I would not read it but was unpopular with my teacher and my parents told me not to take such an attitude. We are told to keep ourselves pure, so what advice would you give me?

ANSWER

You are quite right that the Bible emphatically teaches that we should keep ourselves pure and unspotted from the world (James 1 v 27). Positively we are urged to think on the things that are honest, pure and lovely (Philippians 4 v 8). These are things done in darkness of which it is a shame ever to speak (Ephesians 5 v 11, 12). Much literature contravenes these principles and sad to say some Christian books do as well.

As for your specific problem you are quite right to remain true to principle. Mr Michael Barry, Senior Lecturer in English at Queen's University, Belfast, has pointed out that there are nearly always alternative books that can be selected for study. You can insist on this. Of course, in these circumstances the teacher has every right to refuse to teach outside his selection of books, and you must be prepared to study on your own. You will certainly find that those who honour the Lord, He will honour.

THE CHURCH

QUESTION

Is the church an essential part of the Christian religion?

ANSWER

Unfortunately, we think of the church as a rigid organisation, often centrally governed, making largely irrelevant statements through its national talk shops, housed in antiquated buildings, meeting every Sunday to go through a ritual at which our attendance is obligatory. The New Testament concept of the church is quite different. Wherever a group of believing Christians meet that is the church — so that you have the church in somebody's house. They meet on the basis of relationship — to the Lord and to each other. They meet not because they have to but because they want to. God gives to such a body elders with different gifts (teaching, pastoral care, evangelism) who are responsible for the spiritual welfare of the community. It is a joy to meet as a member of such a church, continuing in the apostle's doctrine, fellowship, breaking of bread and prayers. We have urged not to forsake the assembling of ourselves together as the manner of some is, but to provoke one another into love and good works, and so much more as we see the day approaching. Attending a church building or attaching yourself to an ecclesiastical group does not make you a Christian, but when you become a Christian you want to meet with fellow believers.

QUESTION

Does a Christian have to go to church?

ANSWER

No, a Christian doesn't have to go to church any more than a married man has to live at home — but it is a very odd thing if he doesn't. Here are some good reasons for church-going:

1. Because God has specially promised to meet you there. 'Where two or three are gathered together in my name, there am I in the midst of them, (Mat. 18 v 19).

2. Because you follow the example of the Lord Jesus. He regularly attended the synagogue service on the sabbath.

3. Because the fellowship of God's people is the best fellowship on earth.

4. Because to stay away is to disobey the word of God. 'Let us consider one another to provoke unto love and good works; not forsaking the assembling of ourselves together, as the manner of some is; but exhorting one another; and so much the more as ye see the day approaching' (Heb. 10 v 24, 25).

5. Because otherwise you are not dealing fairly with your brothers and sisters, leaving them to carry your part of the church work as well as their own.

6. Because by your absence you deny them of the contribution your fellowship can make. Be a 'twicer' not a 'oncer' each Sunday, if you possibly can.

7. Church-going will make you happier, wiser, healthier and more honest with God, with your own soul and with Jesus.

QUESTION

How should a young convert not attached to a church, choose one?

ANSWER

1. Find a Bible-believing church where the gospel is faithfully preached.

2. Ensure that they have a prayer meeting and Bible study.

3. Look for signs of spiritual life with a real concern to reach out for souls.

4. Avoid extremes.

5. Take advice from older Christians who exhibit spiritual concern (in the multitude of counsellors there is wisdom).

Having found such a church don't go along with the idea of just receiving. Put yourself out to join in the life of the church. Help in the activities, befriend the lonely, seek to be a blessing in an unobtrusive way. In other words go to give, not to get. And if they have a formal membership, *join* the church. In an age of free milk and orange juice an irresponsible attitude all too easily spills over into church practice, where we take the blessings without being willing to shoulder the responsibilities.

QUESTION

How concerned should a local church be if it doesn't see any converts from one year to the next?

ANSWER

We should be very concerned if we don't see converts from one year to the next. We should examine ourselves to see what sin or slackness is in our lives. We should seek a burdened concern in the prayer meeting. We should overhaul our methods to ensure that we have adapted our methods to a changing culture without diminishing our clear-cut preaching of the gospel.

At the same time we recognise that every spiritual work is a work of God. He gives the increase. Our task is to be faithful. Our rejoicing is not that devils are subject to us, but that our names are written in heaven.

The truth of the last paragraph, however, should never diminish our zeal for evangelism. We need to be like David Brainherd, missionary to the Red Indians, coughing up blood from tuberculous lungs, as he cried 'O God, give me converts or I die'. We need the driving concern of the apostle Paul, 'I could wish myself accursed for my brethren Israel's sake'. We need the compulsion of the Lord Jesus as He exclaims, 'I must needs go through Samaria', and again, 'I must work the works of Him that sent me while it is day, for the night cometh when no man can work'.

QUESTION

Evangelicals are so dogmatic and sure of themselves! What advice can you give to someone who cannot feel so sure and hates the idea of committing intellectual suicide to go along with their ideas?

ANSWER

1. The dogmatism of evangelicals is not based on their own ideas, else it would be arrogance.

2. It is based on a humble submission to the authority of God. It does not exalt human reason above divine revelation.

3. It is not intellectual suicide to take an evangelical viewpoint. The evangelical position is based on overwhelming objective evidence in relation to God's written Word, the Bible, and God's Living Word, Jesus Christ.

4. Never forget that Christianity is not a matter of faith; it is a matter of fact. Christian experience is not a leap in the dark; it is a leap into the light.

5. My advice to the person you cite is to remember that Jesus never asked men to swallow unreservedly His teachings. He said, 'If any man wills to do my will, he shall know of the doctrine whether it be of God or of man.' If a person sincerely seeks, he will find. In particular, take John's Gospel. Read it carefully, thoughtfully, and prayerfully. Many a person has come to faith through reading that Gospel. 'These things are written that you might believe that Jesus is the Christ, and that believing you might have life through His name.'

QUESTION

Can local churches offer any kind of practical assistance to young unemployed people in their area? Any suggestions?

ANSWER

This is one of the greatest problems of this decade, and is likely to become worse. It is a social need that should exercise us greatly. The solutions are not easy, and the pitfalls are many. I know the National Young Life Campaign is setting up a working party to give depth of thought to the problem. Incidentally, it doesn't only affect young people, but it is here the tragic consequences are often greatest.

It is worth defining why unemployment should be viewed so gravely. The unemployed person loses dignity because they lack purpose and routine. Their personality disintegrates and anti-social behaviour may result.

Here are some constructive thoughts. Firstly, as far as the unemployed Christian young person is concerned, we should point out this presents a unique opportunity for service. They can be 'full-time workers' on the state! If a church has a paid worker (eg pastor), he should regard it as a priority to mobilize this force. My suggestion would be for the whole group to meet at 9 am each day from Monday to Friday in the church. Have a time of prayer and Bible study (it doesn't have to be the pastor who speaks every time — nor indeed a formal talk — it could be a short discussion Bible study, sharing what the Lord has given each member from their Quiet Time). The tasks of the day can then be delegated. Some will be practical — digging the church garden, decorating, producing the Church News sheet, folding it, (ie the tasks that are often done by the busiest of people of the church). Other jobs which time had prevented you doing can also be undertaken. (eg duplicating the church notices for distribution on Sunday). Other tasks will be directly spiritual — eg distribution of Challenge newspaper, visiting the elderly and the sick, supporting the Tuesday lunchtime open air meeting in the pedestrian precinct if you are in Leeds! The group may also be involved in helping the unemployed, non-Christian youth, which is a bigger problem, but is a potential opportunity also.

May I say that I doubt whether laudable attempts to substitute cottage industries are likely to make much impact on this issue. (Although I hasten to add that anyone who attempts to tackle the problem in any way deserves our support.) Involvement in social work with voluntary organisations is an obvious constructive outlet. The British Rheumatism Association and Help the Aged are two that spring to mind. The full time minister could offer to co-ordinate and liaise on such efforts. He may also wish to contact the Social Services in this respect. Thought could also be given to additional recreational activities during the day such as football and putting the church hall to good use (most of our church premises are grossly under-utilised).

It may be argued that such co-ordination is no part of a minister's work. That would be a difficult position to sustain. Involvement in the spiritual and social needs of the community should be a deep concern of pastors. The personal contacts these activities would give with young people would be crucial and spiritually beneficial. Moreover it would earn the good will of the community. We need to do all in our power to break down the barriers created by the prejudices of some non-Christians and the hypocrisy of certain church-goers. Goodwill can often be transmitted into souls saved. The discipline and effort this task would involve is a real challenge, and will stretch the pastor spiritually. Backed up by the other elders and the prayerful members of his church, he could achieve a real spiritual triumph.

QUESTION

What are your views about Holy Communion?

ANSWER

May I firstly say some things which the Holy Communion is not.

1. It is not a re-enactment of the sacrifice at Calvary. This of course is a fundamental error of the Roman Catholic Church. The bread is not turned into the body, and the wine is not turned into the blood of Christ. Transubstantiation is heresy. This is why the reformers referred to the blasphemous idolatary of the mass, and died for that principle. The error of transubstantiation is based on a misunderstanding of the phrase, 'This is my body'. At the passover feast when the Lord's supper was instituted the disciples would have no doubt of its meaning. In the passover it is said 'This is the bread of affliction which ours ate in the wilderness'. Of course it wasn't literally so — else it would have been very stale and mouldy. They knew it meant represents. In the same way I produce a photograph from my pocket and say 'This is my wife'. In the same way Paul says 'For this Hagar is Mount Sinai' (Galatians 4 v 25). Whatever the size of the lady she could scarcely be called literally a specific mountain! The cup of the Lord cannot be His literal blood, else those who joined idolatrous sacrifices and took the cup of devils would be drinking their blood (1 Corinthians 10 v 21). The whole error of transubstantiation is in conflict with the teaching of Hebrews, which clearly teaches that the Sacrifice of Calvary is never to be repeated (Hebrews 7 v 27, 9 v 24-28).

For a fuller treatment of this important subject read H. M. Carson's *Dawn or Twilight*?; a study of contemporary Roman Catholicism, published by Inter-Varsity Press (compulsory reading for all those seeking to help Roman Catholics).

2. The communion table is not therefore an altar. Our American friends are wrong in referring to 'an altar call'. The last altar was on Calvary.

3. The one who conducts the communion is not a priest. No special qualifications are required for the one who distributes the bread and wine.

4. The communion is not a special means of grace. The blessing of the Lord's table is in obedience.

Having looked at the negative, here are some positive points.

1. The communion is one of two visual aids the Lord enjoined (the other is baptism). It speaks vividly to us of the price paid by the Lord Jesus for our redemption.

2. It is to remind us of Him. The Lord knew most of us have better 'forgetteries' than memories and we need constantly to be reminded of Calvary.

3. For this reason it should be regular. In my view the ideal is each Lord's day.

4. It is a command of Jesus — so Christians should be at the Lord's table. It is not an optional extra. It was a mark of the early Christians that they continued in breaking of bread (Acts 2 v 42).

5. It is a remembrance for Christians — so the partaking is for them only. But this is the only barrier — the idea of members of one denomination not being able to join at the Lord's table of another denomination makes a mockery of the New Testament doctrine of the church.

6. It proclaims the Lord's death. For this reason at our church we encourage all to stay, and those who are not Christians to pass the emblems. Several Chinese who are Buddhists do this, as well as English who are not Christians.

7. We should not participate in any unworthy manner (1 Corinthians 11 v 29). Many earnest Christians have worried about this verse because of misunderstanding. It does not mean that we are to be worthy in our own selves — the very communion teaches us we cannot be! It must be seen in the context of a church who had degraded the Lord's supper to a drunken orgy, combining it, as they did, with a meal. The chapter was a correction to this abuse — hence my rendering the phrase 'drinks in an unworthy manner', which is what it means.

QUESTION

Is church membership necessary for every believer? How do you decide which church to join?

ANSWER

1. At the moment you become a Christian you **are** a member of the church, the body of Christ.

2. As such you have a loyalty to the Lord **and** to your fellow-Christians.

3. It is logical to express the loyalty to fellow-Christians by being identified with a local fellowship — and indeed it is difficult to see how you can fulfil this loyalty without identifying yourself in such a way. Students are particularly reprehensible in this matter, flitting about from church to church, sermon-tasting. This is to be deplored. It is selfish and unscriptural.

4. It might be said in passing that 'the local church' in Scripture is portrayed as the believers in a town or city, so the above considerations should not lead to a narrow parochialism that never joins with other believers of different denominations.

5. It is all too easy to accept the privileges of the church without shouldering the responsibilities. In a welfare society where children were brought up on free milk and orange juice, this take-all give nothing attitude can spill over into church life.

6. The early Christians continued steadfastly in the apostle's doctrine, fellowship, breaking of bread, and prayers. They obviously were bound in a group of believers, receiving and giving in a learning, worshipping, witnessing community.

7. Where a church has a formal membership, therefore you should apply to join.

8. Some churches do not have a formal membership — that appears to have

been the New Testament situation. In that case get stuck in just the same.

9. It is most irksome to find a church situation where the church business meeting is full and the prayer meeting is sparsely attended. Official members seem able to rearrange their programme to talk business, but not to pray earnestly. Don't be like these. One such business meeting I observed fell on the day grouse shooting began — very appropriate sometimes.

10. Some churches hold their business meetings in conjunction with the prayer meeting. That has much to commend it. The place of prayer makes a good situation and atmosphere to discuss business.

11. In summary. Yes, do become a church member. Be sure your membership is real and contributory, not a name on a roll. Don't forget your responsibilities to the wider local church of the town where you live.

As to which church to join, follow the example of the early believers. Go to a church which preaches apostolic doctrine, i.e. where the Bible is believed in its entirety, where there is a correct view of Christ in His virgin birth, and deity, when the substitutionary atoning death of Christ features largely in the presentation of the gospel, where His literal resurrection and its implications are taught and where His second advent is believed, among the other great truths of scripture.

Go to a church which has a prayer meeting, and go to one where the Lord's death is remembered in the communion. There may be other less important issues which you would wish to have practised depending on your view of whether infants should be christened or believers baptised, of whether you favour a centralised, hierarchial system of church government or a congregational responsibility with oversight by elders of whom one or more may be the pastor(s), and of whether you would desire a charismatic form of worship or a more traditional service. These are peripheral issues not to be compared in importance with the first criteria.

In general terms a local fellowship is to be preferred. Sometimes, however, social factors play a part. You may have been converted through a friend and it is natural to wish to attend their church. Longstanding loyalties to a fellowship may be maintained even after moving location. Nevertheless it reflects no credit on Christians to travel many miles to sit at the feet of a great preacher, passing on the way evangelical causes that struggle for lack of support.

QUESTION

Why do so many odd people come to Christian gatherings?

ANSWER

This is one of the finest commendations of a Christian group. If a Christian fellowship doesn't have more than its fair share of odd people there is something sadly wrong. Among us they should find a love and understanding, a tolerance and concern which is denied them elsewhere. The church above all is a compassionate society. In Adullam's cave it was an odd bunch that David attracted — the debtors, distressed and disgruntled (1 Samuel 22 v 2) — but out of these God was to make an army of mighty men.

We should never forget that 'not many wise men after the flesh, not many mighty, not many noble are called; but God has chosen the foolish things of the world to confound the wise; and God has chosen the weak things of the world to confound the things which are mighty; and base things of the world, and things which are despised, has God chosen, yes, and things which are not, to bring to naught things that are' (1 Corinthians 1 v 26-28).

QUESTION

What is the biblical position on the roles of men and women within the Church and how important it is?

ANSWER

1. For men and women we should all be doing what we can while we can for the Lord. 'Flat out until we pass out!'

2. The modern feminist movement is a product of atheistic humanism. When its members suggest that the Bible and evangelical Christians regard women as inferior, it maligns them.

3. Wherever the Bible has gone it has lifted the status of women.

4. The Bible does not portray men as superior and women as inferior. Before God they are equal, but they are different.

5. The Bible gives great dignity to women. Two Old Testament books are named after women — Ruth and Esther. In the New Testament Paul feelingly refers to certain women as 'fellow labourers in the gospel'.

6. But generally speaking God has equipped the sexes for different roles. The man has a role of leadership (with its attendant responsibility and answerability) and teaching.

7. The role of women in moulding society is apparent in the Bible and in history. The influence of Jochebed on Moses and of Timothy's mother were obviously profound. 'The hand that rocks the cradle rules the world' is still true.

8. There are obvious exceptions to these generalisations. Deborah took a leading role in the affairs of Israel and gave Barak a well-deserved kick in the pants. In foreign missionary situations one would have to say in scores of instances, 'the women is the man for the job'.

CHRISTIANITY

QUESTION

What's so special about Christianity? Won't any religion do, as long as I am sincere?

ANSWER

A man may be sincere, but sincerely wrong. He may be genuine, but genuinely mistaken. I had a patient with severe arthritic pain that stopped her sleeping. I gave her some pills to relieve her pain, and a hypnotic to help her sleep. Two weeks later she returned to say the pain was just as bad, and she was drowsy all the day. She had been taking the hypnotics during the day, and the pain relieving tablet at night! She was sincere but only got worse. Paul said about his own people, 'My heart's desire and prayer to God for the Israelites is that they may be saved. For I can testify about them that they are zealous for God, but their zeal is not based on knowledge. Since they did not know the righteousness that comes from God and sought to establish their own, they did not submit to God's righteousness' (Romans 10 v 13). They were sincere religious people, but not saved.

The uniqueness of Christianity lies in a number of areas.

1. In the world's religions at large you have men reaching up to God. Because that is a desirable thing, you will find some truth in all religion. In Christianity, however, you have God taking the initiative and reaching down to man. He reveals Himself in a double way, through a written word, the Bible, and through a living word, Jesus Christ.

2. Jesus Christ is unique among the founders of religion. He had a miraculous birth; he had a sinless life; he had a saving death; he had a startling resurrection. His coming was foretold centuries before by the prophets of God.

3. Among the unique features above is His resurrection from the dead. Buddha is dead (483 BC aged 80); Confusius lies in the grave (479 BC, aged 72); Muhammad has gone (AD 632 aged 62); Jesus Christ is risen.

4. The world religions are religions of works. Christianity is a religion of grace. Other religions say do your best and try to amass sufficient merit to receive God's favour. Christianity says you can never compensate for the sin of the past however much you try. We would have no hope had not Christ borne our sins in His own body on the Cross. I must flee to Jesus for pardon. Everything necessary for my pardon was done by Him upon the Cross. In the words of Titus 3 v 3 'He saved us, not because of righteous things we had done, but because of His mercy'.

5. Christianity alone gives a man the certainty of heaven. Adherents of other religions hope they make the grade. The Christian trusts a Saviour who says that He will present us before His glorious presence without fault and with great joy.

QUESTION

To what do you attribute the decline of Christianity in England this century?

ANSWER

A number of facts have combined to seduce English people away from Christianity.

1. At the end of the last century, modernism (liberalism) began to emerge from German theologians. This undermining of the truth of the Bible by exalting human reason above divine revelation infected the theological colleges. This process has continued, so that I know of no University Department of Theology and few Religious Education Departments in Teacher Training Colleges which are not destructive. When men do that which is right in their own eyes, it produces a famine in the land. The result of abandonment of biblical truth has been moral bankruptcy in the nation, empty pews in the churches, and personal futility among the majority.

2. At the same time as the emergence of modernism, the evolutionary theory was popularised by Darwin and Huxley. In a day of explosive advance in scientific achievement this was eagerly seized by many in the scientific establishment and by philosophers. The inevitable progress of man was taught on this basis, and forms the basis of most political theories. Man would become the captain of his soul, and the master of his fate, it was taught.

3. For some time the Christian edifice remained impassively intact. But the foundations had been torn away. With two world wars many were taken from families and traditional restraints. Then the building crashed.

4. As a substitute for the absolutes of Judaeo-Christian teaching, existentialist philosophy was substituted. In this system of thought, subjective experience becomes the final arbiter rather than objective truth. Ethics are then determined not by reference to divine revelation, but to the prevailing situation (they are sometimes called 'situational ethics'). Dr Francis Schaeffer has analysed this disastrous switch in his series of brilliant books — which despite their difficult language (at times made up by himself!) are well worth trying to master.

5. An affluent society has produced self-satisfaction.

6. We appear to be in the end times when Jesus taught that the love of many would wax cold. No doubt the devil is hard at work, deceiving gullible, sin-blinded souls.

QUESTION

Why are scientists so much against Christianity?

ANSWER

Your basic premise is wrong. If you puruse the list of the Fellows of the Royal Society you would be amazed at how many were and are at least churchgoers. They are certainly not antagonistic to Christianity. Sir Bernard Lovell, the astronomer who for so many years was responsible for the mammoth telescope at Joddrell Bank, was organist at the local parish church. In our university, the Christian Unions have proportionately a greater percentage of scientists than art students. I believe there are two main reasons for this.

The first is that some arts subjects are more subtly yet definitely anti-Christian than science (which is neutral). Dangerous subjects at an undergratuate level are theology (the devil's playground because it casts doubt on what God has said), philosophy (godless theology), sociology and psychology (which commonly start with anti-Christian pre-suppositions such as determinism).

Secondly, the scientist is taught to think rigorously. Since Christianity encourages people to investigate the available data and to put it to the test, this is commendable to the scientist. Many arts subjects are 'soft-centred', are willing to accept viewpoints on much more flimsy evidence and are subjective, governed by the prevailing philosophy of the day.

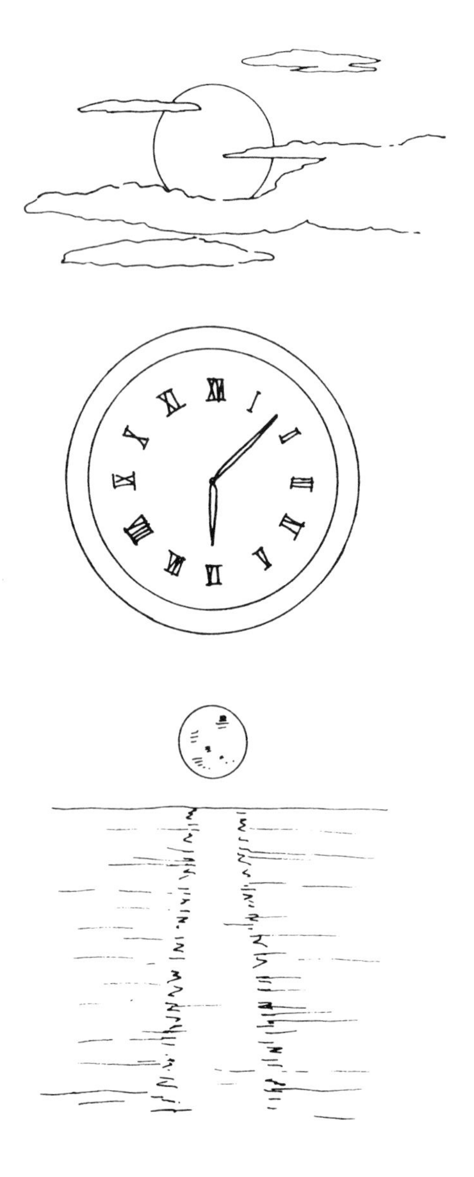

CREATION

QUESTION

What are Bible-believing Christians to make of recent claims about the 'Big Bang' theory of the origin of the Universe? Does it threaten the biblical account of creation?

ANSWER

1. The magazine *Creation ex nihilo* has summarised the 'big bang' as the evolutionary belief that the universe was once compressed into a tiny dot which exploded and from this came, unaided, the entire world of stars, galaxies, planets, palm trees and people.
2. Matter cannot be created from nothing. Order cannot arise from an explosion.
3. The universe is lumpy but background radiation is smooth. There are great walls of galaxies and great voids in between them, so the background radiation (the leftover heat of the big fireball that was supposed to start it all off) should be uneven. But it isn't.
4. The theory had been largely discarded until the recent report by mathematical computation of some unevenness.
5. This unevenness was in fact thirty millionths of a degree. Those who made the instruments are very doubtful if the apparatus is sensitive enough to measure such a small change — it is below the level of instrumental noise.
6. George Smoot, in charge of the project, is not at all sure the effect is real, and adds that even if it is 'it can be caused by other effects, such as the motion of our galaxy through the background radiation.'
7. The Bible clearly states, 'In the beginning God created the heaven and the earth.' Since God was around when the job was done I would expect His Book to give the most accurate account.

QUESTION

Apart from scientific accuracy, what is there in this Evolution Creation controversy to get worked up about? How does it affect the day to day lives of ordinary people?

ANSWER

The implications of the evolutionary theory lie in the doubt it throws on the true nature of man and the need for a Redeemer. The full-blooded advocate of evolutionary theory believes that man is getting better and better and although he has suffered temporary setbacks a race of supermen will one day evolve who will produce a Utopia. The Bible teaches on the other hand that man is fallen and will certainly not get better morally, even though he advances technologically. We must have a literal Adam to stand by a biblical doctrine of sin — 'As by one man sin entered the world and so death passed upon all men.'

Once you remove the truth of man being a fallen creature, you also take away the necessity for a Redeemer and so the logical extension of the theory undermines the atonement as well as the sinful nature of men. This is why the two issues are closely linked in the Bible — 'Therefore as by the offence of one judgement came upon all men to condemnation; even so by the righteousness of one the free gift came upon all men unto justification of life. For as by one man's disobedience many were made sinners, so by the obedience of one shall many be made righteous! (Romans 5 v. 18,19).

QUESTION

How important do you think it is to believe in the literal 24 hour days of creation?

ANSWER

I do believe in the literal 24 hour days of creation. There are good reasons for this. The setting of creation firmly in the historical rather than the poetic section of the Old Testament would indicate that each day should be taken at its face value. Whilst the word 'day' can be used for a long period, such as 'the day of grace', the careful delineation by light and darkness, by evening and morning, strongly suggests a literal 24 hours. Even more important, the 4th of the ten commandments clearly says 'For in 6 days God created the heaven and the earth and all that in them is'. Since God was around when the job was done, and He gave this revelation directly, bypassing even man in the writing of it, you would think He had an idea of the timescale! It is the basis of the Christian week, which comprises 7 literal days.

On the other hand sincere Christians have taken alternative views. I have to say that I think they may have done so because they have given 'science' equal or more weight than scripture without realising the limitations of 'science'. For all that, I respect the alternative views even though I don't agree with them. Dr Scofield believed each day was a long period. This is a modern view, although there is a suggestion that Augustine may have held this. Dr Campbell Morgan advocated the gap theory — in which he believed that between the first and second verses of Genesis 1 there was a long gap. That where it said, 'The earth was without form and void', it could be rendered, 'The earth *became* without form and void'. Professor Wiseman, archeologist, felt that God revealed Himself in seven days.

For a further discussion of these differences I recommend 'Creation and Evolution' in the series *Where Christians Differ* edited by Dr Burke, published by IVP — three creationists and four evolutionists discuss their views.

EMOTIONS

QUESTION

Is jealousy always wrong? For example, a wife's reaction to her husband's affection for another man's wife. Is pride always wrong? For example, the feeling in a job well done, or a good ambition achieved as the result of hard work.

ANSWER

Jealousy cannot be always wrong because in the Ten Commandments God says, 'Thou shalt not make unto thee any graven image, or any likeness of anything that is in heaven above, or that is in the earth beneath, or that is in the water under the earth: thou shalt not bow down thyself to them, nor serve them: for I the Lord thy God am a jealous God, visiting the iniquity of the fathers upon the children unto the third and fourth generation of them that hate me; and shewing mercy unto thousands of them that love me, and keep my commandments' (Exodus 20 v 4-6).

Love is exclusive — and rightly so. Because God loves us, He requires our unreserved loyalty. If we deviate from that path, we not only harm ourselves, but subsequent generations suffer because of the atmosphere of spiritual declension we have created. Similarly, a wife has every reason to claim the undivided love of her husband. At the wedding each promised, 'Forsaking all others I cleave only to thee'. If a partner flirts with others, the spouse has every reason to be jealous. Such jealousy is wrong when it is based on unjustified mistrust. It is also wrong if it demands an exclusive attention beyond the warrant of scripture. For instance, if a wife became jealous because her husband was engaged in church activity whereas she wished to monopolise his time completely, that would be wrong.

A sense of fulfilment in a job well done or a good ambition achieved is natural. Man was made by God to be an achiever. The original instructions to first man were to subdue the earth and to replenish it. Pride which is sinful insinuates itself when I fail to acknowledge the origin of any gifts and abilities I possess. The prosperous farmer, who achieved his ambition to such an extent that he could retire early, heard God's condemnation, 'Thou fool,' as he spoke of 'my goods', 'my barns', and 'my soul'. King Saul prospered when he was little in his own eyes. Self-importance produced his downfall. Better to be like the apostle Paul who declared, 'God forbid that I should glory, save in the cross of Christ my Lord, by which I am crucified to the world and the world is crucified to me.' It is the approbation of God, not the applause of men which counts.

QUESTION

Could you advise me how to control a too quick temper?

ANSWER

The ability to control a too quick temper is something that many can testify happens as a result of becoming a Christian. It therefore follows that the nearer I live to the Lord the more able will I be to have victory in this area. I must cultivate my relationship with Him.

Some other practical tips are:

1. Hear the matter through, rather than arriving at hasty conclusions.

2. Constantly consider what is best for the other person.

3. Let not the sun go down upon your wrath.

4. Since Jesus is very clear that it is impossible to worship unless you are reconciled to your brother, apology is required. Since it never is easy to apologise, it will be a helpful curb.

5. If there is someone with whom we fall out with any regularity, then make sure we pray for them particularly. Not only is that a blessing to them, but it has a wonderfully softening effect upon our own attitude.

QUESTION

Is it a sin for a Christian to be depressed? I suffer from frequent, often very deep, sometimes long-lasting bouts of depression which I have so far been unable to find either a reason (or reasons) or a way out. I have been a Christian for 9 years and 8 months. This is a difficulty I have had to cope with for 12 years (at least). I am a post-graduate research student in a pure science. I enjoy my work, I get on well with just about every person I meet, and there are no obvious causes in any area in my life. I am searching for the way to defeat my depression and am sure that, with God's working in me, and through other Christians, this will result in victory.

Any practical suggestions of what to do to prevent or lessen these depressive bouts would be most welcome. I'm sure that I'm not the only Christian in this position, and that many others are searching just as I am.

ANSWER

You have posed both a diagnostic and a therapetutic problem. Let's take the diagnostic first.

1. No, it is not a sin to be depressed. Depression is in the realm of the emotion, sin in the realm of the mind and of the will.

2. Depression may be a symptom of sin. After David's adultery with Bathsheba he cried: 'Restore unto me the joy of my salvation.' His sin robbed him of his Christian joy. As Arnold Bennett, the famous novelist, lay dying exclaimed, 'It's all gone wrong, it's all gone wrong.' Despair is the final fruit of a

life of self-indulgence regardless of God.

3. More often depression is not a symptom of sin, and it would not appear to be a sin in your case.

4. Such depression may come from external factors (exogenous) or from internal factors (endogenous).

5. External factors may be largely physical, spiritual (satanic opprression), or a mixture of both.

6. Physical external factors may be overwork, emotional stress, tiredness, loneliness, bereavement, etc.

7. Satan may oppress the spirit of a Christian — and may often use the sort of factors above to do so, particularly in creating a sense of failure. Job is a clear example of a godly man oppressed by Satan. C. H. Spurgeon speaks of 'the minister's fainting fits', and speakers are familiar with post-preaching blues, after they have poured out their hearts in proclaiming the gospel.

8. Internal factors in depression relate to our personality. We have swings of mood. If we were 'on top' all the time, we would probably generate so much steam the boiler would burst! If the swing down becomes pronounced we enter the trough of depression. Should the depression become unduly deep or prolonged, and be accompanied by other symptoms that is pathological. It is a disease and must be treated as such.

That leads on naturally to discuss the treatment.

1. If depression is due to sin, then Psalm 51 points the way back. Read it a number of times and make it your sincere prayer. Then rejoice in the promise of 1 John 1 v 7 that the blood of Jesus Christ, God's Son, cleanses us from all sin.

2. Some external depression is natural, cannot be avoided and indeed is part of a good God's provision for all men in a fallen world. The depression often associated with bereavement is an example. This is a valley the bereaved person has to tread. However much we rejoice in a loved one being with the Lord, the physical pain of parting takes its toll. Time will heal the wound. Fellow Christians must be sympathetic and supportive, and not just in the weeks immediately after death.

3. Elijah provides a striking example of external factors at work — he had endured an intense spiritual emotional experience on Mount Carmel with a large element of conflict; he had been saddened by Ahab's rejection of the Lord's work, despite overwhelming evidence of the power of God; he had endured Jezebel's wrath ('hell hath no terrors like a woman scorned'), he had battled alone — while it was true that several thousand had not bowed the knee to Baal, one could well ask where were they?! God's provision for Elijah was sleep, food, fresh air, re-commissioning and a companion.

4. Elijah also exemplifies the element of self-pity. God had to take him to task on that. Elijah had to see that he was not better than his fathers, and in fact things were not so black as he thought (there were other faithful servants of the Lord — thousands in fact).

5. The devil's machinations must not be overlooked. We need to claim victory in that respect. This battle lies in the spiritual realm. The armour provided to thwart his attacks must be taken (Ephesians 6). The Saviour's victory must be claimed, 'Jesus Christ was manifest that He might destroy the works of the devil'.

As the Salvation Army chorus puts it:
'Jesus is stronger than Satan and sin.
Satan to Jesus must bow.
Therefore I triumph without and within
For Jesus is saving me now.'

6. Sometimes in our depression we must have a straight talk to our soul. 'Why art thou cast down O my soul?' The late Dr Martin Lloyd-Jones deals with this admirably in his book 'Spiritual Depression'.

It is helpful to recognise that out of depression may come deepened spiritual experience. Many of the great saints of God experienced depression — it drove them to recognise that their sufficiency was of God. The Song of Solomon speaks of coming out of the desert leaning on the arm of the beloved. However you went into the desert, you will only come out leaning on the arm of the Beloved.

8. Should your depression be of such a depth of duration that it is a disease. YOU MUST CONSULT YOUR DOCTOR. This is particularly so if you realise that during such times you do not have insight into your condition, or if you have feelings of persecution, or if you feel so unworthy or guilty that you feel you want to do away with yourself. One of the psychiatric illnesses where much help can be afforded is depression. It is not unspiritual to be ill whether in body or in mind. It is no more wrong to have depression and consult a psychiatrist than it is to have appendicitis and consult a surgeon. I have known several Christians who have been mistakenly counselled into believing that God will necessarily heal their depression apart from medication, have been assured they had received spiritual healing, have abandoned their tablets, and have committed suicide. Such false teaching brings discredit on the Lord's name.

QUESTION

How can a Chrisitan cope with depression or help someone who is depressed?

ANSWER

You must first make the right diagnosis. Depression may be endogenous or exogenous, that is it may be an internal illness or due to external factors. If depression is endogenous medical advice should be sought. It is mistaken spirituality to resort to faith healing when psychiatric help may be required — and it can be disastrous. I know at least two close Christian friends who died needlessly because they were exhorted to have faith, to believe they were healed and to discard their medication. The treatment of depression is one area in which psychiatry has made considerable progress.

On the other hand depression may be due to external factors. Bereavement is an obvious example. The Lord undoubtedly sustains His children as they journey through the valley of the deepest sorrow. But grief is natural and desirable. In grief there may well be an element of depression, the extent of which may be partly determined by the underlying personality. The Lord uses time as the great healer.

Again, sheer physical tiredness coupled with the aftermath of a climactic experience may be responsible. These were the problems that Elijah faced. The Lord drew him to one side, had him sleep for a long time and then fed him. We are unlikely to improve on our Maker's therapy. A contributory factor in Elijah's depression may well have been loneliness. His heartcry 'I only am left' may have had a tinge of self pity, and certainly wasn't true. But where were the 7,000 who hadn't bowed the knee to Baal? They certainly hadn't identified themselves with Elijah.

Companionship and support is a great preventative to depression — and remember it is lonely at the top — Christian leaders need personal friendship as well as others.

It is wrong to say, 'Take a grip on yourself, man', and may be hurtful. For all that, there is warrant in scripture for self-examination at times of depression as long as we do not become morbidly introspective. The psalmist in those circumstances took, as it were, his soul in his hand, held it at arm's length and addressed his soul, 'Why art thou cast down, O my soul?'. He then encouraged himself. 'Hope thou in God'. Pure rationality rarely solves problems, but a long, calm reminder to my depresssed soul that I have every reason to put my confidence in the God who bought me, does not come amiss. I may trust under the shadow of His wing even when I cannot trace His hand. Moreover, I do well to remind myself from His dealings in the past as well as the assurances of His word.

His love in times past
Forbids me to think
In troubles now present
He'll leave me to sink.

In some circumstances depression may be spiritual in nature. Conviction of sin in the unconverted man may produce depression. The only saving remedy is in true repentance and wholehearted faith in the Lord Jesus and His redeeming work. Deliberate disobedience may produce depression in the man of God. It certainly made Jonah sink down in the depths! Nor was his position altered until he called on the Lord and took up his original commission. Even then self-pity and failure to commit himself to the purposes of God in heart as well as in action brought him low again. In these situations God may have to put us through the mill before we come out on top.

There is a tremendous lot to learn about this subject from the experience of Elijah in 1 Kings 19. The factors in his depression were physical exhaustion, mental frustration and spiritual inattention (he looked in, not up). The Lord dealt with the physical aspect, and on the other hand He didn't rebuke Elijah. He restored his confidence and his commission; He got him going, showing that the way to deliverance is not to cut oneself off and wallow in self-pity but to work out a real concern for others.

In summary, make a correct diagnosis. If depression is an endogenous illness seek medical advice. Depression caused by external circumstances may be lifted by time, by rest, by proper feeding, by companionship. Depression may be due to spiritual factors — but don't assume that is always so (this can be hurtful and harmful). If it is many such conflicts may be resolved in the simple words:

Trust and obey
For there's no other way
To be happy in Jesus,
Than to trust and obey.

QUESTION

What happens to a Christian who commits suicide?

Suicide is continually in my thoughts — and not without good reason. Yes I do have salvation, having turned in repentance and faith to God, when 24. I am also a Calvinist, believing firmly in Election.

Next month I'll be 43, and have been a paraplegic since April '52. Because of bed sores I had to have both legs amputated. My aunt who looked after me since I came out of Southport paraplegic unit in Dec. '55 died 20 months ago. Now I'm on my own, spending most of the time in bed. (I have to get up though to make meals etc.)

I suffer terribly from volmary infection (and have poor kidneys). A number of antibiotics don't work — some only seem to partially work. It's just got worse in the last 15 years. Life is truly a misery, and I've no-one to look after me. Some relatives do shopping, ironing, the garden etc. Two of these are over 70. My neighbour pops in morning and night.

On top of all my troubles I now keep getting bruises on my sitting-down part. I didn't use to. This is an added worry, a real worry for a para.

Life seems so full of worries, so much ill health, I feel if it gets too burdensome I'll take a bottle of aspirins. After all I have salvation, and there's only so much worry I can take. And people will say 'Well, he's better off!'

ANSWER

Thank you for your question, coming as it does from the depths of suffering. May I express my deepest sympathy with your problems, which I can certainly understand strains you to the limit. Some of the answer may lie in aspects of medical care, and I will take the unusual course of writing to you directly with the name of the doctor in charge of Young Disabled Units in your area, so that you can discuss this aspect with your own family doctor. It may well be that a good deal can be done to help from a physical point of view.

May I encourage you not to give way to thoughts of euthanasia (self administered or otherwise). 'My times are in His hands', and however hard the going I may trust Him to gather me to Himself in His appointed time. Indeed I wonder if you always feel as you have expressed yourself — there can be times when black depression sweeps over us and we forget the other times when we are happy to live for the Lord, even though in other ways we long to depart and be with Christ which is far better. Paul faced this very dilemma as he languished in a Roman gaol (Philippians 1 v 19-26). He was very restricted in physical movement, but even there by writing and by speaking to those with whom he did come in contact he exerted a powerful influence for Christ. It may well be that there are ways in which you can forward the work of the kingdom even from a wheelchair.

As the Lord enables you in this difficult situation you can be a help and example to those with overwhelming problems. I had a Christian friend, a doctor who suffered from bouts of severe depression — she helped many others with emotional problems who I sent to her.

As well as writing, I will remember you in prayer that the Lord may undertake and that you may experience His incomparably great power for us who believe (Ephesians 1 v 19 v 20).

May I share one other verse which has been a great help to me (Hebrews 12 v 3).

QUESTION

What is the reason for suffering?

ANSWER

People ask this question for one of three reasons: (1) genuine perplexity (2) personal tragedy (3) red herring.

Even though the motives of the third one are unworthy, the same careful explanation should be given as to the first group, but we should not forget that our purpose is to lead people to Christ not win intellectual arguments.

To those with genuine perplexity we may say:

1. Much suffering is man-made. Greed, hatred and immorality are responsible for hunger, wars and many diseases.

2. Suffering is a necessary corollary of freedom of choice. If mankind is free to choose evil, it follows that suffering is likely to follow wrong choices. The alternative is to make mankind automatons. As C. S. Lewis puts it in his book *The Problem of Pain,* 'Try to exclude the possibility of suffering which the order of nature and the existence of free wills involve, and you will find that you have excluded life itself.'

3. God may use suffering to cut us humans down to size — He speaks to us in our pleasures but shouts to us in our sorrows.

4. The world is in rebellion against God, so it is a wonder that we do not suffer more. Since we are bound up in the bundle of life, tragedy will strike Christian and non-Christian alike. Man is born to trouble as the sparks fly upward.

5. The apostle Paul was allowed to suffer 'lest he should be exalted above due measure'.

6. Suffering may be used to refine our Christian character — the dross is consumed, the gold is purified.

To the one who has suffered a personal tragedy, we may well have to say that we do not know the cause of their particular suffering. All we do know is the Lord is not unmoved by our personal sorrows. He was a 'man of sorrows and acquainted with grief'. Moreover, He endured the agony of the Cross, suffering more than anyone has ever been called upon to suffer.

I will leave you with two pieces of poetry. The first takes the imagery of the weaver.

My life is just a weaving, between my God and me,
I do not choose the colours,He worketh steadily.
Oftimes He weaveth sorrow, and I in foolish pride,
Forget He sees the upper, and I the underside.
Not till the loom is silent, and the shuttles cease to fly,
Will God unroll the canvas and explain the reason why the dark threads are as needful in the the skillful weaver's hand
As the threads of gold and silver in the pattern He has planned.

The second is two verses of Robert Browning.

I walked a mile with Pleasure;
She chattered all the way,
But left me none the wiser
For all she had to say

I walked a mile with Sorrow
And ne'er a word said she;
But oh, the things I learned from her
When Sorrow walked with me!

QUESTION

Do babies which are aborted or miscarry go to heaven?

ANSWER

I certainly believe that a foetus has life from the time of conception. Whether the foetus has a soul from conception I cannot say; and if it acquires a soul later, when that is I certainly do not know, This last sentence does not detract from the dignity of human life from the moment of conception — hence the opposition of evangelical Christians to abortion on demand.

Who goes to heaven is determined by their response to light. 'This is the condemnation, that light is come into the world, and men loved darkness rather than light, because their deeds were evil' (John 3 v 19). The unborn foetus has not rejected light, so that if the foetus has a soul it will go to heaven.

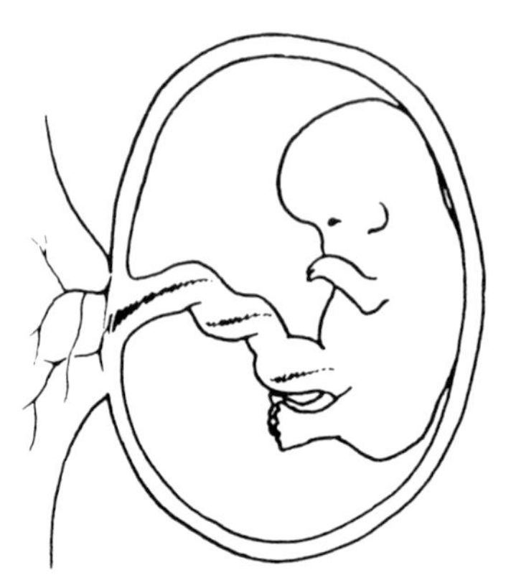

QUESTION

Isn't is a selfish motivation to become a Christian so you can be forgiven and go to Heaven?

ANSWER

You confuse self-interest and selfishness. It is undoubtedly in our self-interest to become a Christian — pardon for the past, power for the present, and provision for the future are undoubtedly worth having, among the many other blessings which accrue to the Christian. Jesus unhesitatingly appeals to man's self-interest 'Come unto Me all you who labour and are heavy laden, and I will give you rest.'

Selfishness is when I benefit at the expense of someone else. That is not so with becoming a Christian. Christ has paid the price, so salvation is free to the repentant sinner. Far from depriving other people, it blesses them. Laban learned that God blessed him for Jacob's sake. So did Potiphar in relation to Joseph. Through the centuries it has been the same. When people become Christians, they have blessed society — hospitals, orphanages, emancipation of slaves, factory reforms, are but a few of the social benefits, quite apart from the spiritual impact of their lives.

QUESTION

In what ways if any, should we be preparing for eternal life now?

ANSWER

We must appreciate the eternal life is something we have now — it continues into eternity (1 John 5 v 13). Some of the things this causes us to do are:

1. Lay up treasure in heaven (Matthew 6 v 20). Remember the lady who on being upset by the small dwelling accorded to her in heaven was told, 'we did the best with the materials that were sent up!'
2. Use your money to win souls then they will be there to enclose you into eternal habitations (this is the moral of the parable of the unjust steward).
3. Count the praise of men a thing of little consequence. Much better to hear the Masters 'Well done, thou good and faithful servant'.
4. Keep under your body, lest having preached to others, you yourself should become a castaway (1 Corinthians 9 v 27).
5. Impart sound teaching to young Christians — it is this which builds gold and precious stones on the foundation that is Christ, and will construct an edifice that withstands the fire of judgement (1 Corinthians 3 v 10-16).
6. Remember you are part of a colony of heaven, that is where your citizenship is — live as such (Philippians 1 v 27).
7. As pilgrims and strangers abstain from fleshy lusts which war against the soul (1 Peter 2 v 11).
8. As pilgrims and strangers live the life of faith (Hebrews 11 v 13) demonstrating to the world that you are a foreigner and therefore, different (in speech, in customs, and at times in dress).
9. Hold with a light hand all material possessions.
10. 'Preach Him to all, and cry in death, Behold, Behold the Lamb.'

QUESTION

When we die will we go first into hell and then on Judgement Day go into heaven?

ANSWER

The short answer is No! The apostle Paul spoke of his desire to depart and be with Christ which is far better (Philippians 1 v 23). The context leaves no doubt that he envisaged an immediate transition. The the dying thief Jesus said, 'Today you will be with me in paradise'. In the incident He recounted of Lazarus and the rich man, Lazarus was in the place of bliss, and there was no passing from hell to thence because of the chasm between.

In 1 John 5 v 13 we are assured that we have eternal life as a present possession — hell is the place of separation (hence of death). Indeed we shall never have to stand before a judgement bar concerned with our salvation. There is therefore no condemnation to those who are in Christ Jesus (Romans 8 v 1). We rejoice that heaven is our home, and we are going straight there at the moment we slip anchor from this shore. Or as our friends of the Salvation Army put it, we are 'promoted to glory'!

QUESTION

A Jehovah's Witness told me only 144,000 would be in heaven, and that number (from among the Jehovah's Witnesses) was now complete. I thought all Christians went to heaven. Which is true?

ANSWER

The teaching about the 144,000 is found in the book of Revelation. Let us assume it is literal, as the Jehovah's Witnesses do (highly unlikely in such a symbolic book). Whatever does it have to do with J.W.s?

1. The 144,000 were Jews (7 v 4-8).

2. They were on the earth not in heaven — the passage starts, ' I saw another angel — and he cried with a loud voice to the four angels to whom it was given to hurt the earth and the sea.'

3. They were men (14 v 3, 4). 'No men could learn that song but the 144,000, which were redeemed from the earth. These are they which were not defiled with women.'

4. Those in heaven are a great throng (7 v 9). 'And this I beheld, and lo, a great multitude, which no man could number, of all nations, and kindreds, and people, and tongues, stood before the throne, and before the Lamb, clothed with white robes, and palms in their hands.'

QUESTION

What will happen to the millions who die, never having heard of Jesus, because you can't be saved by good works.

ANSWER

This question is commonly asked in open air meetings and in personal conversation. Remember these principles:

1. The judge of all the earth will surely do right

2. This is the condemnation, that light is come into the world but men preferred darkness to light because their deeds were evil. Man is judged by his response to light. You and I have had maximum light, knowing of the One Who is the Light of the World. We will be judged by our response to Christ.

3. Their trial will be in a different courtroom from ours. Be grateful.

4. We may leave the verdict safely in the hands of a judge who dispenses perfect justice and who exhibits perfect love.

GOD

QUESTION

Who made God? Is it just a story which everybody is taught to believe?

ANSWER

The short answer is that no one made God — He always has been. It is not just a story which everybody is taught to believe. There is ample evidence for the existence of God in creation, in revelation, and in redemption. However, since the question is so frequently asked, especially among young people, it is worth exploring its logical impossibility.

The sceptic sometimes phrases it, 'Where did God come from?' He starts from two premises: 1. You can't be eternally around without having a start. 2. I don't believe in an original cause. From that he states 3. I don't believe in eternal existence. 4. So once you are dead you are done for.

Let us now put to our sceptical atheist the question of the origin of the universe. There are two alternatives. I. Matter has not always existed — if so, there was a Creator God. 2. Matter has always existed i.e. it wasn't made. The atheist obviously objects to the first proposition because it requires the existence of God. That leaves him with the solution of matter being eternally around without being made. But previously he had said you can't be eternally around without having a start.

In other words, from pure logic the Universe demands the likelihood of an eternal God. That in fact is where the Bible starts — 'In the beginning God . . ' He is the Creator God who has revealed Himself by a written Word, the Bible, and by a living Word, Jesus Christ.

QUESTION

Some people are now saying they think we should call God our Mother as well as our Father. What do you think please?

ANSWER

Jesus taught his disciples to pray 'Our Father,' that should be good enough for any Christian. We do not take our Christian thinking from a feminist movement which has its roots in secular humanism, nor from modernist theological colleges who have abandoned the final authority of Scripture. In Biblical terms the father exercises authority, assumes responsibility, protects and provides. It is, therefore, critically appropriate that God should be called 'our Father'.

QUESTION

How can you as a scientist, still believe in God?

ANSWER

As a scientist I would find it difficult not to believe in God. The fact of creation forcibly suggests a creator, and the evidence of design a designer. Much greater scientists than me have come to the same conclusion, e.g. Faraday, the famous physicist, and Kepler, the great astronomer. It may interest you that in most of our universities the biggest single society is the Christian Union, and the largest number of members come from the science faculties.

The question suggests that you haven't understood the nature of science.

1. Science can only investigate those things open to testing (i.e. it is empirical). As D. Sherwood Taylor, the organic chemist, put it, 'Science does not say Jesus didn't turn the water into wine — only that the phenomenon has not been observed at other times'.

2. Science covers limited objections. It tries to answer the question 'How?', but not 'Why?'. It may tell me how I am made, but not why I am here.

3. Science is forever changing. Each new discovery makes the scientist change his views, sometimes radically. A scientist can never arrive at certainty, nor does he expect to do so.

For these reasons science can never answer the basic problems that confront men, their nature and their future. No scientific formula can mend a broken home and put together a life smashed by sin. Faraday said about the future, 'Science is not equipped to deal with that. The glory of a future world can be known only by revelation.'

Interestingly, to come into Christian experience you follow the lines of scientific methodology. Firstly, you investigate the available data. Secondly, you put it to the test. If you are seeking truth, I would recommend you read John's gospel to look at the facts. You will then come to a point where you will be required to commit yourself to Jesus Christ of whom those facts speak — that is the crucial test or experiment.

QUESTION

I have been a Christian for some 40 years now but the following thought is ever with me:
We believe of course that 'God is love' this is proved in the coming of Jesus but has, or did, God change, as I cannot forget the fact that God once created 'the great flood', this was not an act of love surely?

ANSWER

There are a number of points which arise from your question, that has puzzled many people.

1. We must never think that love and justice are incompatible. It is because I love my fellow men and my country that I want to see law and order upheld, and wrongdoers brought to justice.

2. The wickedness of the people in the days of Noah was overwhelming. The New Testament tells us that those days were characterised by scoffing, carelessness, violence and immorality.

3. The extent of their wickedness is shown by the fact that not one outside Noah's family turned to God when the opportunity was given over scores of years.

4. There comes a time when the only answer to sin is eradication. This step is a kindness of succeeding generations. This drastic yet essential step grieved God (Genesis 5 v 6).

5. A good illlustration of the necessity of such action is well illustrated by a man with a gangrenous leg. No pain is more demoralising. I have seen fine young fellows totally broken by such a catastrophe . . . and have been unbelievably transformed by amputation. The disease which was destroying their personality was removed and they have rejoiced at the radical surgery.

6. Nor were these people left without a chance. In His mercy God called Noah to preach to them for many long and weary hours. None need have been lost. The means of salvation was at hand.

7. Remember too that ultimate judgement which will engulf the whole world is likewise deferred — the certainty of Christ's coming to judgement is linked with the events of Noah's day, and the delay is explained 'The Lord . . . is patient with you, not wanting any one to perish, but everyone to come to repentance' (2 Peter 3 v 2-10).

8. Remember too that Jesus saw nothing incompatible between His message of love and His execution of judgement. He warned men to flee from the wrath to come. He said, 'Except you repent you shall all likewise perish'.

QUESTION

How does God's love differ from human love?

ANSWER

1. God's love never changes. 'He has loved us with an everlasting love.' Human love waxes and wanes.

2. God's love is never selfish. It is often difficult to disentangle the motives of human love.

3. God's love does not depend on what I am like. Greater love has no man than this, that he gives his life for his friend. But it was while we were yet sinners that Christ died for us.

QUESTION

Please would you comment on whether a Christian who suffers in an accident is being judged by God?

ANSWER

Jesus dealt with this issue when he spoke of some Jews being killed by a falling wall. He pointed out that their sin was probably less than that of His hearers. A Christian is just as likely as the rest of mankind to be involved in an accident (except that he probably will not drink and shouldn't exceed the speed limit). The idea that health and freedom from injury are marks of spirituality in a New Testament dispensation is utterly fallacious. I observed that a great friend of mine was more healthy when he was a backsliding Yorkshire county cricketer than he is as an all-out Christian disciple!

In His sovereignty, God can even use injury to His greater glory. Joni Eareckson is a classic example. She is not the first. Dr Mary Verguese of India was a fine dedicated Christian who became paraplegic in a road accident. She comments that God took her legs and gave her wings. She was certainly greatly used from her wheelchair. The suggestion of the question would be an insult to those fine Overseas Missionary Fellowship workers who were killed in Thailand returning to Manoram hospital.

HOLY SPIRIT

QUESTION

What does it mean to grieve the Holy Spirit?

ANSWER

This injunction comes from Ephesians 4 v 30. If the statement is put into context the question is answered. 'Do not let any unwholesome talk come out of your mouths, but only what is helpful for building up others according to their needs, that it may benefit those who listen. And do not grieve the Holy Spirit of God, with whom you were sealed for the day of redemption. Get rid of bitterness, rage and anger, brawling and slander, along with every form of malice. Be kind and compassionate to one another, forgiving each other, just as in Christ God forgave you' (v 29-32).

Boice, pastor of the First Presbytarian Church in Philadelphia, comments, 'The Holy Spirit is chiefly the Spirit of revelation, first giving the Word of God in written form, in our Bibles, and then blessing the teaching of that Word by faithful persons for the building up of the church. The Holy Spirit blesses human words to edification. So it must grieve Him particularly when the speech of Christians, rather than building up the church as it should, is used to tear down others who are part of that body.' The relationship between God and us is a loving relationship. Just as in a home the father is grieved if there is a fall out among the children, so the Holy Spirit is grieved by quarreling and intemperate language among the children of God. The Holy Spirit is happiest in an atmosphere of love, joy and peace, for these are the fruit He produces in our lives.

QUESTION

In these days of confusion about the gifts, etc, how would you advise a very young Christian?

ANSWER

1. Don't get things out of perspective. Teaching about gifts occupies a small part of the Bible. Become thoroughly grounded in the *whole* Bible before you become taken up with segments. It is important that your Christian position should be based on the Word of God, not primarily on experience.

2. Don't be pushed into anything because of pressures of a group or of a friend. Think things out for yourself from the Bible.

3. Leave controversial matters until you know more.

4. Look at the fruits of those who advocate any particular line. (a) Do they preach the Bible, explaining passages systematically? (b) Is their evangelism gospel-centred, not music-centred? (c) Do they live holy lives, separate from the sinfulness of the world, keeping the Lord's day, and daily reading the Bible?

5. When you do come to consider these issues in depth, try to see all sides. Make your starting point, 'What says the Scripture?' Take an historical perspective and look at the emphases of the great men of God down the centuries. Consider the implications doctrinally and practically of each position.

QUESTION

When we hear the promise that the Holy Spirit will guide us into all truth how is it that godly Christian men do not always agree, e.g. on eternal security?

ANSWER

The statement is made by Jesus in John 14 v 26 and we have to recognise the theological limitations of the utterance. It referred to promise of the Comforter who would come, after He had gone. As such it was fulfilled at Pentecost and the apostles were guided into all truth as they penned the Scriptures and gave to us a New Testament of absolute historical accuracy and unerring spiritual counsel.

For today, we have to appropriate human fallibility, the deceitfulness of the heart, the influence of upbringing and the pressures of our environment. It takes a lot of grace to give up deeply rooted prejudices. When I consider how much I had to grow in grace and knowledge before I would shift my ground theologically, it makes me more tolerant of those with alternative views.

QUESTION

For over thirty years I have been agonised over St Matthew's gospel chapter 12 v 32. Can you help me over this unforgivable sin? George Duncan at Keswick told me that as a Christian I had no worries. I quite agree, but my sin is worse, namely, God is a Spirit and we should worship Him in Spirit. The same applies to Jesus Christ. My mathematical mind makes me wonder why have a Holy Spirit if God's Spirit and Christ's Spirit can be called on. I do not mean any blasphemy but I have never had a satisfactory answer.

ANSWER

Your problem is partly experimental and partly theological. Taking the experimental first:

1. In the Old Testament to call good evil, and light darkness, as the Pharisees did, received special condemnation. 'Woe to those who call evil good, and good evil, who put darkness for light and light for darkness, who put bitter for sweet and sweet for bitter' (Isaiah 5 v 20).

2. In the New Testament 'blasphemy against the Holy Spirit' is ascribing to the devil the works of Christ.

3. Any who feel worried about having committed the unforgivable sin may rest assured that they have not. Had they done so they would be hardened and insensitive. The Holy Spirit produces concern, and their very worry demonstrates they are not forsaken.

4. Prof. R. V. G. Tasker, formerly Professor of New Testament Exegesis in the University of London, has a profound comment on Matthew 12 v 22-37. 'Every other sin that men may commit, even

speaking against the Son of Man, could be forgiven, but **not** the sin of him who wilfully rejects the truth when once he has seen it, or who denounces as evil what he knows to be good (31, 32). Peter could be said to have spoken a **word against the Son of Man**, when he tried to stand in the way of Jesus when He was taking a course of action that could lead to His death (16 v 23), or when he three times disowned Him at the time of His trial. But in all this Peter was merely being unstable and inconsistent. He was not deliberately speaking **against the Holy Ghost**; he was temporarily, but not fundamentally, divided against himself. At heart he was loyal, and he remained a disciple, Judas, on the other hand, always acted consistently with his nature; he was permanently in the service of himself and Satan, even while professing to be an apostle. He could be said therefore to be speaking **against the Holy Ghost**, and so he readily became the tool of Satan, and betrayed Him who was bringing in the Kingdom of God in the power of the Holy Spirit. The root of his nature was bad, and therefore the fruit of his character was also bad. Jesus, on the other hand, was radically good, and it was no more possible for Him to be allied with Satan than it was possible for a sound tree to produce bad fruit (v 33).

As far as other aspects of your theological problem are concerned, the problems of the trinity are not solved mathematically. Three persons in one Godhead are as difficult to comprehend as three dimensions of time (past, present, future) being all one to God. We recognise our human limitations and accept the revelation of God. It is ours to rejoice in the love of God, enjoy the grace of our Lord Jesus Christ, and be empowered by the fellowship of the Holy Spirit.

JESUS CHRIST

QUESTION

As far as the virgin birth is concerned: (1) Is it scientifically correct to say 'The conception was entirely the work of the Holy Spirit. Mary was the vehicle of Christ's birth and did not contribute to His being'. (2) 'Because of His virgin birth Jesus didn't have on drop of Jewish blood in His veins'.

ANSWER

It would be difficult to defend the proposition that 'Mary was the vehicle of Christ's birth and did not contribute to His being'. Although scripture states 'a body hast thou prepared me' (Hebrews 10 v 5). It also says how this came about. That which was conceived in Mary was of the Holy Ghost (Matthew 1 v 18-20). Nevertheless Mary conceived the child (Luke 1 v 31), having had the Holy Ghost come upon her (Luke 1 v 25). The conception from a biological point of view seems to have proceeded quite normally from that point — and indeed followed a similar course to that of her cousin, Elizabeth, of whom it also says she conceived (same word, Luke 1 v 24). Elizabeth therefore refers to Jesus as the fruit of Mary's womb (Luke 1 v 42). It is for this reason that Isaiah says in chapter 9 v 6 'Unto us a son is given (Deity; of God), unto us a child is born (humanity; of Mary). The Bible goes out of its way to point out that Joseph was not the father of Jesus, saying 'being the son of Joseph, as it was supposed', (Luke 2 v 23) but makes no such aside regarding Mary.

The fact that the body of our Saviour was prepared via the womb of a woman does not mean the He was sinful in any way, we don't know how original sin is transmitted.

Similarly, it is beyond the bounds of scripture to say Jesus was 'not a Jew by race: He didn't have one drop of Jewish blood in his veins'. The Bible goes to great length to establish his Jewish genealogy. Moreover He readily accepted the title, 'Jesus, thou Son of David'. Biologically if he grew in Mary's womb with a placenta and an umbilical cord, it is difficult to envisage how a cross-circulation would not be established between the mother and baby.

The incarnation of the Son of God was not a diminishing of His deity, but an acquiring of manhood. It was not that God the Son came to indwell a human being, as the Spirit was later to do. It was rather that the Son, in person, began to live a fully human life. He became the man Christ Jesus. (1 Timothy 2 v 5, Galatians 4 v 4, Hebrews 2 v 14,17). Although He lived in a state of dependence and obedience, it was also a state of sinlessness and impeccability (2 Corinthians 5 v 21, 1 Peter 2 v 22, Hebrews 4 v 15, Matthew 3 v 14-17, John 8 v 46, John 2 v 1).

I find it helpful to see the relation between the incarnation and the Holy Spirit's work in terms of God's double revelation — the written and the living Word. With the Written Word, 'Holy men of God wrote as they were moved by the Holy Spirit' (1 Peter 1 v 21); the result was an infallible Word which yet holds the stamp of the style of the author. The human characteristics of his writing were there, (it was 'him'), but he was preserved from error. So, likewise, when the Holy Ghost came upon Mary, the Living Word was born, truly divine and fully human, but yet without sin.

QUESTION

If the way to heaven is narrow and not many go that way, and the way to hell is broad and many go that way, doesn't this mean that the devil has more power than the Saviour?

ANSWER

No, it does not. It is a statement of fact, and demonstrates that our all-powerful God does not treat men like robots who are programmed, but allows men the power of choice. Some would see moral choice as part of the image of God in man. Certainly as C. S. Lewis so vividly puts it, there are only two sorts of people in the world, those who say to the Lord, 'Thy will be done' and those to whom He says, 'Thy will be done'.

The ultimate end of the devil demonstrates that he is not more powerful than God. 'And the devil that deceived them was cast into the lake of fire and brimstone, where the beast and the false prophet are, and shall be tormented day and night for ever and ever.' (Revelation 20:10). Moreover Jesus Christ was manifest that He might destroy the works of the devil. As Bunyan portrays it so well in *Pilgrim's Progress*, the devil is a chained lion as far as the Christian is concerned. Indeed he is a toothless lion to those who walk with the Lord; he may roar but he cannot bite.

Remember that at the end of time all things in heaven and in earth will be gathered up with Christ, not unto the devil. Hebrews 1 v 2 clearly shows that he has been appointed heir of all things. Ephesians 1 v 9, 10 shows that God's good pleasure is 'that in the dispensation of the fullness of time He might gather together in one all things in Christ, both which are in heaven and which are on earth, even in Him.'

QUESTION

If Christ died for sins 2,000 years ago, how can His blood cover sins committed today?

ANSWER

God is outside time and therefore although Christ died in space and time, his atoning death is of eternal significance. That is why He is termed 'the Lamb slain from before the foundation of the World'. Moreover, He is risen from the dead and lives in the power of an endless life, so that He is able to mediate the benefits of His vicarious sacrifice to all who will trust him.

LORD'S DAY

QUESTION

Where does it say in the Bible we should go to a church building on a Sunday? Isn't it just tradition?

ANSWER

1. It does not say in the Bible we should go to a church building on a Sunday, but there are good reasons why we should.

2. That is where Christians gather, and the Bible clearly teaches that we should not forsake the gathering of ourselves together as the manner of some is — and that is especially true as the second coming draws near.

3. Corporate worship is to be commended — the early Christians met on the first day of the week to break bread.

4. It shows we regard Sunday as the Lord's Day, and that we are 10 Commandment believers, not 9 Commandment defaulters.

5. It is a good testimony to our neighbours. It is a great sight in Northern Ireland, for instance, to see the large number of people going to church with their Bibles.

6. The building itself is not sacrosanct and that needs to be stressed — consecrated buildings were a feature of Old Testament worship not New. The New Testament majors on consecrated people not consecrated things. Nevertheless, for convenience we meet in a church building, built for that purpose.

7. Not all tradition is bad — only that which makes of none effect the law of God. There are good traditions and we do well to preserve them. Church-going is one such. And be a twicer, if you can, not a oncer.

QUESTION

Can a Christian take a job that involves working on a Sunday (say a milkman) if he takes a day off in the week and uses this as the sabbath?

ANSWER

The Bible lays considerable emphasis on one day in seven being set aside as a holy day. For the Jews this was the Saturday; for the Christians it has become Sunday — this is our sabbath. As a mark of love to the Lord we will wish to keep this as a special day, particularly in an age when the Lord's day is being increasingly eroded (a factor undoubtedly in the serious problems that beset our country).

At the same time Jesus clearly taught that works of necessity and works of mercy were permissible on the sabbath. Where, however, we can avoid working on a Sunday we should. If the sole motive is more money then this is certainly a wrong motive. In the case of a milkman, I would either work for a dairy that delivers double on a Saturday (many do) or seek a job elsewhere.

QUESTION

Remembering that Sunday is the Lord's Day, can you make some positive suggestions of ways to spend the day?

ANSWER

1. Apart from your personal devotions, your first priority is to join with the people of God. 'Don't forget the assembling of yourselves together as the manner of some is. ' Be a 'twicer' at church, not just a 'oncer'. Too many Christians seem to think they have done their duty to God by putting in a single appearance at church. No wonder they are tempted into activities no different from the world careless of spiritual things.

2. To walk in God's countryside is a pleasurable Sunday activity — walking through a lovely garden does cause us to praise the Creator. Not that the world's adage, 'You are nearer God's heart in a garden than anywhere else on earth', is true — it was in a garden that Man first rebelled against God; it was in a garden that the Saviour sweated drops of blood; it was in a garden that He was crucified.

3. Sunday is a good day to read Christian books. The busy schedule of the week often prevents this.

4. Many a missionary on the foreign field would be blessed if we spent some time on Sunday writing a newsy letter to them.

5. Visiting relatives, lonely folk and needy people will be a profitable exercise in the less pressurised atmosphere of the day of rest.

6. Don't forget to invite lonely folk to Sunday lunch — especially single members of the church family, the widows and fatherless (this is part of the essence of pure religion, says Jesus).

7. Remember also to invite needy ones to tea, so that you can take them to church in the evening.

8. I write the answers to the questions asked in this column on a Sunday afternoon! You might like to write a paragraph for your church magazine. That would surprise the editor!

RELATIONSHIPS

QUESTION

What tips do you have about Christian courting?

ANSWER

1. Develop your relationship in the right order.

2. That means your first priority is to develop your spiritual relationship, the next at an emotional (personality) level, and thirdly at a physical level.

3. Much of the last should be in the bonds of marriage.

4. In the biography of the evangelist, Gypsy Smith, he comments that all gypsy courting must be done within sight of the prospective mother-in-law! And adds that gypsies have one of the highest rates of marital fidelity.

5. Do things together to serve others.

6. Do not be selfish in your courting. Consider not only the other half, but the half that doesn't have another half.

7. That is one reason why I recoil at seeing young people hugging each other, and draped across each other in church or other fellowship meetings.

8. Major Bill Batt, evangelist and convention speaker, used to go up to such couples at University Christian Unions and ask them if he could help them. They were usually furious — but the next day the girl would often come to seek his counsel.

QUESTION

I have felt led recently to go out with a non-Christian boy. What else do you think I should do to win him for Christ?

ANSWER

The first thing to do to win this young man for Christ is for you to give him up as your boy friend. Wherever your 'leading' comes from, it certainly does not stem from God. God has declared His mind on this matter in no uncertain terms, saying that we should not be unequally yoked with the unbeliever and that light has no fellowship with darkness. Two cannot walk together unless they are agreed. Since God is not self-contradictory, it follows that your feelings have mis-led you. God never guides contrary to what He has said in His word.

Every Christian conversion is a work of God, and the important thing is that you should be in the place of power with God and with men. The principle of answered prayer in the first place is that there should be no unconfessed sin between you and God. 'If I regard iniquity in my heart, the Lord will not hear me'. By maintaining your friendship with this young man therefore, you have put your self in the place of spiritual powerlessness, where God will not answer prayer. You must rest assured that if he is the young man for you, once you are walking in obedience to God's will he will fulfil His perfect plan for you — and if that plan includes this young man you will ultimately be linked together.

QUESTION

What do you think about a couple who are going out together, going camping together? Or youth hostelling? Do you think it's wise?

ANSWER

The three basic principles I must follow are:

1. I need to recognise my own weakness. Each man who stands must beware lest he falls.

2. I must distance myself from temptation as far as possible. Learn from David's great sins. He was at ease on his housetop when he ought to have been with the troops in battle. He allowed his eyes to linger on a beautiful woman undressing. He invited her into his presence. Thus he led himself into adultery and subsequent lying and murder.

3. I should abstain from all appearance of evil.

For the couple you instance youth hostelling seems reasonable, but I would doubt the wisdom of camping together. Tell them to come on a beach mission. They'll get plenty of exercise and fellowship — and there is free time!

QUESTION

If you have a very strong, loving relationship with a person and you're not married why should you wait to have sex? Why is it better not to have sex before marriage? If you do have sex and then get married, why or will things change?

ANSWER

1. In a marriage there needs to be a sense of security. A public and definite commitment to each other with solemn promises made before God in the presence of the witnesses helps to achieve that.

2. There also needs to be trust and loyalty within the relationship. If one of the partners is not prepared to make a public binding pledge, there is always the nagging fear,'what about when he tires of me?'

3. Lack of discipline before marriage is a fertile ground for suspicion afterwards. If the partner is away on business for several days, can he (she) really be trusted? If they couldn't restrain themselves before, will they do so now?

4. True love loses the consciousness of time. Jacob worked seven years for Rachel, 'and it seemed but as a day for the love he had for her'.

5. The best reason of all is that this is God's plan, and His way is always the best way. He withholds no good thing from us.

6. You ask, 'what will change?' Many people have found that to go to bed together before marriage as you are suggesting is like opening a Christmas present before Christmas Day — it takes away the sparkle. I know of several marriages which have quickly become stale, because the partners committed themselves to each other physically before they could give the other the honour, loyalty and total care a marriage bond allows.

QUESTION

What help can you offer to Christians who are homosexual?

ANSWER

1. We must recognise that homosexual practice is sinful, however much tolerated by the laws of our permissive society (Romans 1 v 27).

2. We must not minimise the gravity of this sin, much less condone it as a natural variation.

3. On the other hand, we must not adopt a holier-than-thou attitude, because we do not have problems in this realm. Our personal sins are just as heinous.

4. Homosexual tendencies are not sin, any more than other temptations are sin. It is only when we succumb to lust that it is sin.

5. The blood of Jesus Christ, God's Son, cleanses us from all sin (1 John 1 v 7) — and that includes this sin.

6. The homosexual needs to avoid the place of temptation. The company of other such men is not helpful.

7. As far as he can he needs to avoid anything which would inflame these desires.

8. Coupled with that he needs to avoid all appearance of evil — so he would be ill-advised to work with an all male young people's group.

9. He needs to nurture his spiritual life — by study of the Bible and by fellowship with God's people, especially in prayer.

10. He needs to be active in the service of Christ. The devil does find work for idle hands to do.

11. He needs to seek daily the Holy Spirit's power to gain the victory in this area of pressing temptation. Remember the Old Testament ritual of how the blood was put on the extremities, and then the oil was applied. What the blood cleanses, the Spirit Himself fills.

QUESTION

Do you think homosexuality is due to a disorder of the genes?

ANSWER

There is no evidence that homosexuality is genetic. The suggestion is sometimes made to excuse a sinful, perverse practice. It infers that the person cannot help it, and it is inevitable. That is certainly not true. Paul writes to the Christians at Corinth; 'Don't you know that the unrighteous shall not inherit the kingdom of God? Don't be deceived; neither fornicators, nor idolators, nor adulterers, nor effeminate, nor abusers of themselves with mankind, nor thieves, nor covetous, nor drunkards, nor revilers, nor extortioners, shall inherit the kingdom of God. *And such were some of you;* but you are washed, but you are sanctified, but you are justified in the name of the Lord Jesus, and by the Spirit of our God.'In other words, among those converted and changed at Corinth were those who had indulged in homosexual practices.

That is not to say that we should not sympathise with those who have problems in this area. But we all have temptations to which we are particularly prone. The same principles in combating temptation apply to all potential sins regardless of their type.

QUESTION

Does the Lord call some people to be single?

ANSWER

God's best plan for most people is to marry. but not for all. Jesus gives clear teaching on this in Matthew 19 v 10-12.'His disciples said unto Him, if the case be so with his wife, it is not good to marry. But He said unto them, All men cannot receive this saying, save them to whom it is given. For there are some eunuchs which were so born from their mother's womb, and there are some eun-cuhs which were made eunuchs of men; and there be eunuchs, which have made themselves eunuchs for the Kingdom of Heaven's sake. He that is able to receive it, let him receive it.'

An outstanding example of this in church history is Charles Simeon. For 54 years he was a Fellow of King's College, Cambridge, and vicar of Holy Trinity Church. At that time you couldn't be a fellow of a college and marry. In order to maintain his position of spiritual influence in the university he deliberately remained single. MacCaulay says of Simeon that he was a greater influence for Christ than any Archbishop of Canterbury has ever been. Likewise, the foreign mission field testifies to the incredible impact that single lady missionaries have made.

QUESTION

How far does a wife's submission go? Should she have to follow every detail her husband wishes? What do you feel an attitude should be to Women's Lib, etc?

ANSWER

The Bible's teaching is plain — the man is the head of the home and should assume that responsibility. The fact that the wife is to submit establishes an important principle in the type of man to whom a girl should say 'Yes'. It will be that man in whose Christian character she has such confidence that she doesn't believe he will ask her to do anything that she wouldn't wish to. Submission then equals doing what I want, which is always pleasant! It means the man will be a Christian. It means he will be spiritual. It is not then a question of subservience but agreeing together. The fact that the husband has ultimate authority does not preclude discussion — and the persuasive wisdom that most wives exhibit has a bearing on the exercise of that ultimate authority! If a man is the head of the home, then the woman is often the neck, which determines to a considerable extent the direction in which the head is turned!

I believe Women's Lib is essentially anti-Christian: The Christian gospel has exalted the position of women to its rightful place that no other philosophy has. The subjugation of women under Islam for instance, is frightening. Christianity brought women into the true role of being complementary to man. Not under his feet to be subjugated, not on his head to rule, but out of his side to be embraced and cared for! Women's Lib is a reflection of humanistic philosophy with its overthrow of Biblical standards. While it may have redressed a few legitimate grievances, it has robbed women of the due care and honour which is their rightful due. The Bible does not teach that women are inferior, it teaches they are different. So much of Women's Lib with its strident accompanying cry of 'emancipation through the pill' is a product of our permissive society.

QUESTION

I am about to ask a good Christian girl out. However, I am concerned that if marriage results I might become tired of her after a number of years.

ANSWER

You should wear a notice 'Girls beware', until you have appreciated the essence of marriage, although I realise your question is a natural result of the philosophy of the day. You might, incidentally, ask more relevantly and humbly, 'Will she grow tired of me?'

I commend the following points to you:

1. Marriage is for keeps — it is 'till death us do part'. The ink of the marriage certificate is of a special type which does not fade throughout a lifetime.

2. Marriage 'is for better or for worse'.

3. Marriage is a solemn contract and the Bible has dire warnings for those who break vows.

4. Love is not merely emotional. It contains a large element of the will.

5. *Choose your love, and love your choice.*

6. If you are not prepared to seek the Lord's will for your life's partner and enter into such a union with the above principles in mind, then you shouldn't think of going out with a girl.

QUESTION

If a young wife feels she wants to come to Christ, but her husband is violently opposed, what should she do?

ANSWER

Come to Christ. There is nothing more important in this world or the next than a person coming to Christ. Jesus taught that except a person hates those who are dearest to them he cannot be my disciple. By that Jesus didn't mean a dislike, but rather that our love for Him must transcend all human loves. Moreover, if a wife truly loves her husband she will want the best for him. The best is obviously that he should become a Christian. That is more likely to happen if she trusts Christ herself, then lives a transformed life before her husband, so that he sees the reality of Christian experience before his very eyes. That is why in 1 Corinthians 7 v 13 and 17 Paul says, 'And a woman who has a husband who does not believe, if he is willing to live with her, let her not divorce him . . . For how do you know, O wife, whether you will save your husband?' She will make her impact by her practice rather than her preaching.

QUESTION

Many Christians today have lived immorally before conversion. Can such a person marry? In what circumstances could he or she not marry?

ANSWER

This problem was rife among the early church. Speaking of the immorality which characterised the pagan society in which they lived Paul says 'and such were some of you'. In coming to Christ they could know that the blood of Jesus Christ God's son cleansed from ALL sin (1 John 1 v.7). There is no suggestion in scripture that such cleansed sinners should not marry. Indeed, rather the reverse in that the Bible teaches it is better to marry than to burn (1 Corinthians 7 v 9). The only circumstances to stop a person marrying would be if they were married already.

QUESTION

How do you like someone you don't get on with?

ANSWER

You are not told to like anybody in the Bible, but you are commended to love them. To love someone is to desire their highest good and to act accordingly. You will find that as you do that your feelings toward them change. But the first thing is to set your will — and there is much more of that will in loving than is usually recognised.

Secondly, you should pray for them, especially if they despitefully use you. Again you will find that praying for someone else has a remarkable effect on your attitude to them.

QUESTION

I am working in a company with quite a few bosses. Every year they have an interview with the personnel officer, the section head and the individual worker. You are told to express your opinions about the section head. I have been working there for 3 months. What do I do about it if judgement is wrong?

ANSWER

You are not correct to say 'judgement is wrong'. The Bible tells us to shun vain and profaine babblings. That involves a judgement of substance. We are bidden to provoke one another to love and good works, and to exhort one another 'while it is called today lest any be hardened through the deceitfulness of sin'. That involves a judgement of persons. You see this in Galatians when Paul withstood Peter to the face because he was to be blamed.

It is obviously your firm's policy to have this expression of opinion about fellow staff members. You may be sure your bosses will express their opinion about you — and rightly so. Every time I write a judgement for someone I am 'judging' them. It is inevitable. Since staff members are all familiar with the firm's policy it is up to them whether they accept it, or indicate their rejection by resigning. Implicit in their beginning the job is their acceptance of the company's policy. The situation you describe keeps the bosses in line!

I take for granted, of course, that the Christian does not gossip or backbite. May I make the following additional general points:

1. We cannot be blind to, or if appropriate fail to mention, glaring faults. To con-

tenance extra long lunch hours, sloppy work, etc, is to have double standards.

2. If work is adversely affected, or if it is serious enough to talk about, then you should talk directly to the guilty person. But that is not to be done lightly — it is not your place to be an active office conscience. If you have an understanding colleague, talk it over with him first.

3. If you are the boss, it is your job to deal with faults for the firm's sake, in fairness to the rest of the staff, and for morale.

4. If the management have a personal reporting system, be fair and give credit where credit is due.

5. Don't speak out of personal grudge or irritation.

6. Be aware of your own weaknesses, as well as those you talk to.

7. Don't take the initiative in belittling someone.

8. Never believe rumour, stick to fact.

9. Be understanding of the person's problems that may have contributed to the fault.

10. Always balance their good points.

11. Don't go on and on; change the subject.

12. Act out of a desire to help — or else keep quiet.

13. Be prayerful.

QUESTION

How humble should a Christian be when applying for a job?

ANSWER

1. In applying for a job a prospective employer expects you to put yourself in the best light. There may only be a little in the shop, but at least you can make a good window display!

Recently I interviewed a man for a medical post. After school he had done two years on a farm, and one year on the buses before returning to technical college to get appropriate A levels and then make a career for himself in medicine. He had omitted all that from his application form. We advised him to insert it in future. It reflected great credit on him that he had shown such determination.

2. Remember however that employers can usually see through exaggeration.

3. What is worse is that if you do deceive, when reality dawns in the harsh light of employment, the next reference you get is likely to be damning. Similar to 'this man has performed his duties entirely to his own satisfaction'!

4. Stick to facts. Honesty is commended in Scripture, is consistent with Christian character and pays in the long run.

5. In these circumstances humility is not undue modesty (which is no help to an interviewer, but as always is a willingness to abase myself for the blessing of others.

6. You may trust the Lord to see you get the right job.

SALVATION

QUESTION

Do you really think there is any lasting value in 'instant' conversions?

ANSWER

Every true Christian Conversion is a work of the Holy Spirit. Whether this is instant or protracted is immaterial.

'The vilest offender who truly believes that moment from Jesus a pardon receives.'

It must be recognised however, that even conversions which appear to be 'instant' are usually preceded by a convicting work of the Holy Spirit. To all appearances Paul's conversion on the road to Damascus was instant, but there is no doubt he had been long rebelling against the ox-goad's of conscience, and who would doubt that profound effects of witnessing Stephen's death. Moreover, there is the solemn warning of the parable of the Sower in which we see that the seed which springs up quickly often has little root and is of no enduring value in that, when the heat of persecution comes, it withers. This was a superficial response and although a conversion in the sense that there had been a turning, was not a Christian conversion in the sense that there was a deep work of the Spirit of God with the seed of the Word of God deeply implanted in the heart. It is rare for there to be a harvest without preliminary ploughing, sowing, and watering but none can dictate the ways of God — 'The wind blows where it lists.' The important lesson is to await spiritual fruit before we assess professed conversion. We are ill-advised to chalk up decisions as examples of Christian conversion. Time shows.

QUESTION

Can one be saved without knowing it?

ANSWER

1. Salvation is of the Lord. In the final analysis it is the Lord who knows those who are His.

2. It is normal for someone who is saved to know it. Jesus said, 'I am the good shepherd and know my sheep, and am known of mine' (John 10 v 14).

3. Anyone who is saved would know there was a difference in their lives. When the Spirit of God works in our lives it is a radical change, and His Spirit witnesses with our spirit that we are the children of God (Romans 8 v 16).

4. A person may be saved without enjoying the certainty of salvation.

5. This arises from lack of Bible knowledge or from defective teaching. Interestingly you may see it at two ends of the spectrum. I have met Roman Catholics who gave every evidence of the work of grace within their heart and they appeared to be trusting wholly in the merits of the redeeming blood of Christ, yet of course their system of church teaching precludes certainty. At the other extreme, godly Puritans often went through agonising struggles before arriving at certainty. Reading their biographies, including that of John Bunyan, this needless anguish seemed to be due to a faulty understanding of faith, and of how we could rest on the promises of God, regardless of feelings.

QUESTION

I wonder if you can explain Hebrews 6 v 4, 5 & 6, as my daughter is depressed as she thinks she has committed this sin and has no hope of being forgiven and is bound for Hell.

ANSWER

The first thing to say is that no one who feels concerned about their spiritual state has committed the unforgivable sin. That sin is blasphemy against the Holy Spirit and in consequence the Holy Spirit withdraws all His influence. Since conviction of sin is a ministry of the Holy Spirit it follows that this is no longer felt. Anyone, therefore, who is troubled about their sin or their hardness of heart exhibits a working of the Holy Spirit and cannot have committed the unforgivable sin.

It was a mistake into which the puritans were prone to fall. John Bunyan in 'Grace Abounding to the Chief of Sinners' tells of the times when he was sure he had no hope of being forgiven because of the very feelings your daughter experiences. His glorious Christian contribution subsequently is eloquent tribute to the fact that this was not so.

You must appreciate that the epistle to the Hebrews was written to the Jews. My own view is that they were never saved. As a nation God has blessed them greatly — they had the scriptures, so in that sense were enlightened (God revealed His Will and His Way to them). They had certainly tasted the heavenly gift, since they had been recipients of God's bounty. They had been partakers of the Holy Ghost (the sense is 'to go along with') in that with the Jewish people they had experienced the gifts, operations and influences of the Holy Spirit. Likewise they had tasted the good word of God and, in that they had witnessed the miracles, had tasted the powers of the world to come. Having rejected these manifestations there is no other way back to God.

There are those who believe that these verses are purely hypothetical in view of the phrase 'if they shall fall away'. Verse 9 strongly suggests that those to whom the previous verses refer were not Christians, since it says, 'But beloved we are persuaded better things of you, and things that accompany salvation'.

SOCIAL AND MORAL ISSUES

QUESTION

What should be the Christian's attitude to abortion?

ANSWER

It is important to appreciate what the law was and what it has become since the opinions of the group mistakenly called the Abortion Law Reform Society prevailed. The law allowed gynaecologists to perform an abortion for strictly medical reasons, e.g. if the mother's life was at risk by the birth (a mother with severe heart disease might die during pregnancy or labour). Now, the terms of the law are such that it requires little difficulty to have a situation not far short of 'abortion on demand'. It was in this way, London became known as the Abortion Centre of the World. Such attitudes contribute to the permissive society which is corrupting our country. It is interesting that when I was asked recently to represent our Regional Health Authority at a conference of hospital chaplains on a question panel, many liberal chaplains openly said that whilst they had supported the new Bill, now they saw how it had worked out in practice their views had changed completely. It is also of profound significance that gynaelcologists as a body were opposed to the Bill. The government saw fit to ignore this body of professional opinion from doctors who would have to implement the changes — opinions given from a professional concern and care for patients, not for any motives of self-interest.

It is easy to think that abortion solves an immediate problem. This is dubious — the statistics on how many promiscuous women rapidly become pregnant again are frightening. But even if it were so, it would not justify a code of practice

QUESTION

Do you think AIDS is caused as punishment from God or from evil?

ANSWER

There are a number of important points to make.

Both are true. God has set boundaries of human conduct. If we transgress those which are placed there for our good (just as a fireguard is placed before the fire not primarily to restrict a child but to protect him), we are highly likely to suffer. Wage war on nature, and nature will wage war on you. Turn to evil, and evil will bring vengeance. Pour alcohol down your throat, and your liver will rot. Inhale tobacco smoke continuously, and your lungs will be destroyed. Indulge in homosexual practice and you are highly likely to contract AIDS. There is an inevitability about the laws of God. What you sow, you reap. Your sin surely finds you out.

2. God has established a correct procedure for sexual practice. Stay within the circle of a married relationship and you will be blessed. Stray outside it and you will perish.

3. It is reprehensible that the church has not uttered a firmer condemnation of homosexual practices. When the evangelist Roger Carswell mentioned at a recent University Mission that homosexual behaviour was sinful, his meetings were picketed by the Anglican Chaplaincy. He was vilifed as a 'gay basher'.

4. Homosexual practices are wrong. Let us make no mistake about it. It is sad the government's million pounds programme to educate the public about this fearsome disease carries no moral emphasis.

5. We may have sympathy with someone

whose temptations lie in this area. But we can no more condone these practices than we would those of an adulterer, or a thief, or of a murderer.

6. We need to see the problem in perspective. Many people were concerned as they saw the emaciated form of Rock Hudson, dying from AIDS. We need to be even more deeply worried about an entrenched moral attitude of opposition to God in people dead in sin.

QUESTION

Is it right for a Christian to donate or receive organs from another person, who may be dead or alive? This involves blood transfusions it seems to me.

ANSWER

The inference of your question is that blood transfusion is wrong. This is the position of the Jehovah's Witnesses and is based on a misunderstanding of scripture. In the Old Testament it was forbidden to eat blood to emphasise the importance of the blood — 'the life is in the blood'. (The point is beautifully brought out, incidentally, in the excellent Fact and Faith film 'Red River of Life'.) This in turn was a foreshadowing of the central importance of the blood of Christ — 'it was not with perishable things such as silver or gold that you were redeemed . . . but with the precious blood of Christ' (1 Peter 1 v 18, 19). We are not redeemed by the life of Christ but by His death (the life outpoured — the shed blood). In the New Testament the Gentile believers were required to abstain from blood, but the letter from the Council of Jerusalem suggests that this was in relation to idolatrous sacrifice. 'You are to abstain from food sacrificed to idols, from blood, from the meat of strangled animals and from sexual immorality' (Acts 15 v 29). I would have no hesitation therefore in receiving a blood transfusion, and I would encourage people to be blood donors (it is a small act of service to our fellow men that we can render).

Similarly, I would have no hesitation in donating an organ — in fact you have pricked my conscience and I will get a kidney donor card to carry, which I've been meaning to do for some time. When I'm gone to glory anyone may have such bits of my vacated house (body) as they wish. I'm looking forward to moving into new premises! Some Christians have worried about the ethics of parting with their heart. The heart which should be our major concern is not the physical one, which is a remarkable pump, but the centre of us which is referred to metaphorically as the heart. When we speak of 'losing our heart to someone' we do not envisage a saping hole in our chest (even though the ulitimate consequences may be a gaping hole in our pocket). This is a vivid, descriptive term as metaphorical as the phrase 'bowels of mercy'.

QUESTION

How do you detect a cult? A Mormon comes to our Christian Union and I have good fellowship with her. What should I tell her? I don't like to cause friction.

ANSWER

Firstly, may I say that at times friction is inevitable. When you stand for truth, friction will inevitably occur in this situation. We must earnestly contend for the truth. Ensure, however, that it is the truth which causes the friction, and not an abrasive attitude on our part.

A cult denies fundamental doctrine — many have in common that they deny the deity of Christ, the substitutionary atonement of Christ, the eternal punishment of the wicked, and salvation by faith alone in the finished work of a once crucified, now risen, Saviour.

The niceness of your Mormon friend must not woo you. Remember the devil is a deceiver, and his ministers may appear as angels of light. The French have a proverb that, when the devil was younger, he was a handsome fellow. He still is in some of his guises.

You might care to ask your Mormon friend whether their founder, Joseph Smith, was a false prophet. If not, how does she explain that in his writings Joseph Smith said the moon was peopled by men over six feet tall. We now know that this is false! Then ask whether the next in line (after the movement had split — a fact they are at pains to hide, since their great argument is, that Christendom is divided), Brigham Young, was a false prophet. He wrote that people lived on the sun! With succeeding generations the tales got bigger and better! For further information consult *Echoes of Utah*, produced by Pastor John Cuthbert. At the same time remember we are not out to score points but to win these needy, misguided souls to Christ.

QUESTION

Jesus tells us 'owe no man anything but love.' Should Christians take this literally, as the unavoidable result would be that mortgages are not to be taken out, no bank loans etc? Would the Lord provide if we take Him at his word?

ANSWER

If you have a mortgage, you do not own your house; the building society does until you have paid! That is the agreement into which you entered, so it is not relevant to the general principle you raised.

1. As a general principle do not get into debt. Proverbs teaches that if we fall into debt we become servant to the creditor.

2. If you must borrow, see that you have enough capital to repay the loan.

3. Learn to be thrifty. Don't be cajoled into getting things because you want them. Don't yield to the mass materalistic, despicable slogan of the Westminster Bank Access Card system, 'It takes the waiting out of wanting.'

4. Don't buy what you cannot afford.

5. You can ask the Lord to meet your every need, not to provide a surplus.

QUESTION

Why is drug taking frowned upon by the Christian Church? Smoking and drinking alcohol is practised by many Christians and many drugs are far less harmful than these.

ANSWER

The Church frowns on drug taking because the Bible teaches that man should care for his body. We are the creation of God, and should not abuse that creation. This is why the death penalty was prescribed for the violation of the sanctity of human life (Genesis 9 v 6). For the Christian his body is the temple of the Holy Spirit and therefore he should not desecrate it (1 Cor 3 v 16,17). This is why we cannot condone smoking, although we may sympathise with those gripped by the habit.

The second reason for deprecating drug taking is on the basis of experience. Many have found it ruined their body and their mind. For those indulging in mild drugs there is always the danger of escalation — this is in part due to the drug culture in which drugs may be taken. The Christian is concerned to achieve reality, not fantasy. He considers truth more important than 'happiness'.

It is of interest also that drug taking is often associated with witchcraft and experiences of the occult. These things are an abomination to the Lord. (Deut. 18 v 10-12).

QUESTION

Is euthanasia biblical and is it biblical to have a life-support machine switched off?

ANSWER

Euthanasia is not biblical. Three men in the Bible asked for their lives to be taken away: Job, Elijah and Jonah. None of them tried to kill themselves and in no case did God grant their request. 'Our times are in His hands.'

There are good medical and sociological reasons against euthanasia — which is why the British Medical Association is opposed to it. The clamour of a few for it often derives from needless fear of terminal suffering. One of the great contributions of the hospice movement, introduced into this country by the fine Christian lady, Dame Ciceley Saunders, has been to show the medical profession how you can relieve pain without clouding consciousness. Another has been to emphasise death with dignity.

As far as a Christian is concerned, there is a testimony to be borne in dying. Death is the last great enemy and it is one of the unique testimonies of a Christian that Christ has gained the victory over it.

The doctor's task is to cure where possible, to rehabilitate when function is limited, and to alleviate suffering. Whilst it is never his mandate to kill, neither is it his responsibility to prolong needlessly the act of dying.

QUESTION

What is the Christian viewpoint on euthanasia, especially as the subject is debated openly in the US at the moment and a book on how to commit suicide is a best-seller?

ANSWER

The Bible clearly teaches that our times are in His hands. There are many practical reasons to reject the practice of euthanasia:

1. It erodes trust between doctor and patient.

2. It opens the elderly and weak to pressure from unscrupulous relatives.

3. The desire may be the manifestation of depression, which will lift later. Many a person in the depths of despair has had momentary desires to end it all, which have passed as their spirits have lifted. But euthanasia is irreversible!

4. It violates the primary purpose of the doctor — to save life not to destroy it. That I may say is different from officiously keeping alive. The prolongation of an elderly person's life for a few hours by painful medical heroics is not part of a doctor's brief.

5. People are unaware of the great contribution to medical care of the dying by the hospice movement (intiated in this country by the fine Christian lady, Dame Ciceley Saunders). We are able largely to relieve pain without clouding consciousness.

From a Christian point of view it should be noted that no one who asked God to take their life in the Bible had that prayer answered (Elijah, Job and Jonah). Moreover, there is a powerful testimony to be borne in dying. A wonderful recent example was provided by Jill Johnstone whose obituary appeared in a recent issue of *Evangelism Today*.

QUESTION

Should a Christian continue their freemason activities? 'Is freemasonry incompatible with Christianity?'

ANSWER

I can't answer this question from personal inside information, but suggest that freemasonry appears to be incompatible with a dedicated Christian walk for the following reasons:

1. At a practical level it results in an attitude of 'you scratch my back, I'll scratch yours'. This may mean I do not deal fairly with my neighbour.

2. It requires the taking of non-essential oaths. This may mean holding secrets from the family, which is never desirable.

3. Although the members of the cult acknowledge the great architect of the universe (one sometimes wonders whether the god they truly worship is mammon!), masons are not allowed to promote their religious point of view if others are present. In other words, your Christian witness is muzzled.

4. The symbolism and myths associated with the cult owe little to truly Christian origins. They are much more linked with Rosicrucianism.

The few freemasons who have been converted with whom I have spoken have all advocated leaving, indeed the most outspoken have made two points to me. Firstly, it is amazing what fools unconverted men may make of themselves. Secondly, have nothing to do with it.

QUESTION

I am wondering whether you have ever had to deal with what to me is a real puzzle, gambling. I have never put a penny on a horse or a dog in my life, I deplore my grandchildren being taken to races where they see it going on, but I have been accused of gambling because I bought some shares in a company and put money into industry. There must be a moral difference. Is there a doubtful element in all the free prizes being offered by, say,* **Reader's Digest**, *the A.A. and even Cancer Research? If there is I could never define it.

ANSWER

Your question is an interesting one because it covers the whole spectrum of this issue — from black through grey to white! The issues as I see it are:

1. Gambling is wrong. It is a social evil which has brought ruin to many. Even more important it is a violation of God's law — the tenth commandment says 'Thou shalt not covet'.

2. For that reason football pools, lotteries and gambling on horses, dogs or the roll of a dice is to be deplored.

3.The irritating way in which *Readers Digest* clutters your mail with offers of huge prizes by returning stickers, and hopefully buying the book or record they advertise at the same time, is not strictly gambling in that you pay no money directly. Of course, someone does ultimately — they are not a philanthropic organisation and somewhere along the line the purchaser pays. I would not therefore classify this as wrong. But I do regard it as the thin end of the wedge, and dump such mail in the waste basket.

4. The fact that a worthy cause uses man's covetous instinct to raise money (e.g. by raffles) does not make it right. We do not do evil that good may come thereby. So I don't purchase such raffle tickets. Nor do I give a donation to the person in lieu, since that merely makes that particular money-making ploy appear to be a success. I do, however, say I will make an independent donation, and do it directly to the cause.

5. You can gamble on the stock exchange — and I would regard this as equally wrong.

However, industry needs capital to develop and shares are a perfectly legitimate way to raise that money. The investor is putting his money to work. Jesus condemned the man who buried his talent, telling him that at least he could have loaned it out with interest. The alternative way of making your money work is of course to put it in a deposit account in a bank — where they promptly invest it in shares that make more money for them! Banks are not philanthropic institutions either! So I wouldn't have a bad conscience about your shares — I hope it is a good company and that you do well. You will then have money to give away.

QUESTION

How would you deal with someone who accuses God of being callous and doing nothing about the starving children in Africa? People often say, 'If He is all-powerful, why doesn't He do something?'

ANSWER

Many of the problems for which God gets the blame are man-made. Ten years ago a carefully documented book warned of the impending famine in Ethiopia. The government of that country chose to spend its money on armaments instead of taking positive measures, and still to my amazement levies import duty on the shipments of grain to the starving thousands. Get-rich-quick attitudes of farmers have ignored basic principles of conservation. Corruption at many levels siphons much needed aid into the pockets of unscrupulous profiteers (hence the wisdom of directing help via agencies in which you have confidence, such as missionary societies and Tear Fund). Nor in the Western world are we blameless — while mountains of beef lie unsold in Europe, we can hardly point an accusing finger at God for failing to meet the need of starving children in Africa.

The dilemma about asking God to intervene is where does He stop His intervention? Sin is the root of many of these problems, so logically God would have to go down the line dealing with sin in each offender — which includes you and me. God *has* in fact done something. He sent his Son to die on the cross to forgive our sin, made available the Holy Spirit so that Christ by His risen life may indwell us.

The prime fruit of the Spirit is love. That is why down the centuries the great charitable institutions have nearly always been motivated by the love of Christ. Countless millions of sufferers have cause to bless Christ for the relief His followers have brought.

However, let it be said that God will intervene once more, definitely and finally in human history. When Christ comes again to reign, these problems will be finished. But remember, when the author walks on the stage, the play is over. We need to be ready to meet the King — having yielded allegiance to Him, so that as loyal subjects we may welcome Him and be owned by Him.

QUESTION

A number of questions have been asked about demon possession. Is it a reality? Does it occur today? How is it discarded? What is the place of exorcism? Is there a good book on the subject?

ANSWER

Ouija board, witchcraft and other trappings of spiritism, have become big money. Even in the Christian world there has been an unhealthy interest in the occult, and judging by some sensational publications the profit motive may not have been entirely absent here either. For all that, these issues have to be faced squarely, since spiritism may derange mentally, deform physically, debase morally and destroy spiritually. Moreover, as the case in 1975 from a Yorkshire church which resulted in murder and suicide, indicated much discredit can be brought on the work of God by delving into this realm inadvisedly.

A good book on the subject has recently been published by the Banner of Truth, entitled *Satan Cast Out: a study in biblical demonology*. Frederick Leahy, the author, is a pastor in the Reformed Presbyterian Church of Ireland. The first 59% of the book is a comprehensive, balanced exegesis of scripture. The author demonstrates clearly that while there is the danger of holding exaggerated views of Satan's authority and power, it is just as dangerous to regard him as of little or no consequence. Bunyan's illustration of the chained lion remains one of the most explicit.

Demon possession does occur, but compelling evidence is advanced to suggest that a Christian cannot be demon-possessed. As far as discerning demonic presence, the author is particularly helpful. 'There is not one technique for "ordinary" sinners, and a special technique for "demon-possessed" sinners. It is not the responsibility of the Christian worker to decide definitely that a person has or has not a demon. That is a knowledge possessed only by his Master and in proclaiming His name the missionary or counsellor has obeyed the Lord'. At the same time we are warned against having an attitude to the name of Jesus which borders on magic. Well-meaning Christian workers sometimes feel that they should follow the practice of commanding demons in the name of Jesus to depart. But if there is no experience of salvation through the preached Word, what has been accomplished? There is no biblical evidence to believe that the name of Jesus was ever meant to be used for merely medical and therapeutic purposes.

This volume has biblical depth and is a study book. It is tough going at times and all the better for that. This is not a subject with which to pander to the sensational. It is far too serious and potentially dangerous. No one should approach it unless they are prepared to dig deeply into scripture first.

QUESTION

How can you advise an unemployed teenager to use their time during the day? Please give practical suggestions.

ANSWER

1. Keep trying to get a job — any job. I know some teenagers who will not take a job because it is 'beneath them'. Abandon that philosophy. A friend of mine in his 40s was made redundant. He couldn't obtain a job at all in keeping with qualifications, so he took a job as a sweeper in a supermarket. In two years he was the manager.

2. Ask the pastor or another of the elders what work there is to do in the church.

3. Study for a qualification.

4. Plan and structure your day strictly. Beware of idleness.

QUESTION

Are riches wrong for a Christian?

ANSWER

The Bible does not say that riches are wrong, but it does stress that they are deceitful. They bring very great problems and temptations. Indeed the love of money is the root of every kind of evil. It is all too easy to trust in riches and for our life to revolve around them. The thrust of the Bible is that we should not lay up for ourselves treasures on earth. There is a place for saving for limited objectives, and business men may require money as a tool of work. But there is no doubt that riches can so easily bring a creeping paralysis, and a reluctance to share. Our problem is not to rise, but keep down. Possessions are a cramping thing, and the thing we must ask ourselves is 'are we emptying or are we accumulating'. There can be no doubts that our Saviour was one who emptied himself, and if we wish to walk where Jesus walked, we shall heed his example.

QUESTION

How does one gain a concern for the lost?

ANSWER

This is God given. The closer I live to the Lord Jesus the more I shall find myself constrained by the love of Christ. He saw men as sheep without a shepherd and had compassion on them. If He lives in me and possesses me, then His love will flow out of me as rivers of living water. Negatively, remember that entanglement with the things of the world will dim my love for the Saviour and for the lost world He loves. Positively, I will be helped by involvement with a concerned fellowship — not one that is inward-looking but one that looks up and out. It is also a great encouragement to get on and do the work of an evangelist. There are few thrills to equal that of leading souls to Christ.

QUESTION

If, after asking for forgiveness over sin in one's life, the peace of forgiveness does not come as expected, what does it mean?

ANSWER

We must differentiate between peace with God (that is salvation) and the peace of God (that is experience). Peace with God comes when I turn from my sin in real repentance and turn to Christ for pardon. It happens regardless of how I feel, since it is the peace treaty to which God appends His signature in blood.

The peace of God will surely come in due course as I appreciate what Christ has done for me and as the Holy Spirit makes His presence felt. One great Christian wrote, 'I looked to the Lord and the dove of peace flew in. I looked at the dove, and it flew out again'. Our first concern should be to look to Jesus, and to follow Him as closely as we are able. As we obey His word we will find He manifests His peace to us.

A relevant section on experienced peace is found in Philippians 4 v 6-13. It teaches that peace is obtained through prayer (v 6, 7) through positive thinking (v 8), application of the word of God (v 9), and through the provision and providence of God (v 11-13,19).

QUESTION

Although I am a believer in our Lord Jesus Christ, I sometimes feel that God is far away from me. I suspect I may not be alone as a Christian in having these feelings and would value your advice for myself and all who seek a closer walk with God.

ANSWER

Rejoice that the nearness of God is not dependent on our feelings, but on facts. In counselling someone who has just trusted Christ we sometimes use the illustration of the three boys who played follow-my-leader. They were called Faith, Facts and Feelings. Inititally Feelings led the way, but they were soon in the ditch. Then Faith went to the front, but again they landed in the nettle patch. They only made progress when Facts led the way. Faith looked to Facts and Feelings followed on (sometimes he lagged a long way behind, having short legs. but he always caught up). That illustration of the basis of Christian certainty is relevant all our life.

Moreover, there are considerable dangers in an excessively experienced-based Christianity. In times of trouble such believers are often terribly shaken. They have tied their faith to emotions, which may be catastrophically upset by external circumstances over which they have little-control, so that in the crisis hour they have not learned to rely on the rock solid facts and promises of God's Word.

Sidlow Baxter has a lovely account, reproduced in the Young Life magazine, *Quiet Time*. 'There was a part of me that did not want to pray. But there was a part of me that did. The part that didn't was the emotions and the part that did was the intellect and will.' He describes the two and a half weeks' battle he had as Will took him to prayer. 'Then one morning as Will and I were going to prayer, I heard one of my chief emotions say to the others, 'Come on fellows, there's no use wearing ourselves out; they'll go on whatever we do.' Three weeks later while Will and I were pressing our case at the throne of the heavenly glory, one of the chief emotions shouted 'Hallelujah!', and the other emotions shoulted 'Amen!'. For the first time the whole territory of James Sidlow Baxter was happily co-ordinated in the exercise of prayer and God suddenly became real and heaven was wide open and Christ was there and the Holy Spirit was moving and I knew that all the time God had been listening.'

The promise is still true, 'Draw near to Me and I will draw near to you'. The basic rules of Christian living are still the best advice for a closer walk with God. 1. Forsake sin. 2. Cleave in obedience to Christ. 3. Cultivate His friendship in Bible study and prayer. 4. Meet with fellow Christians that we may be provoked to love and to good works.

There are special promises in the Bible about the closeness of God. Hebrews 11:13-16.

QUESTION

How can I plan a Quiet Time?

ANSWER

1. Buy an alarm clock.

2. Set it in good time to have a Quiet Time at the start of the day.

3. As you hear it exclaim 'I love my Master. I will not lie in bed.'

4. Translate thought to action and get up!

5. If at all possible find a quiet place alone.

6. Having selected a definite place, make a definite time. Bad habits should be shunned but good habits fostered. Let this time be an ingrained habit of your life. Discipline is not opposed to spirituality, it is the root of discipleship.

7. Read a portion of the Bible.

8. Be systematic in your Bible reading. Don't despise helpful aids like Scripture Union notes.

9. Have a prayer time.

10. I recommend it to be on your knees. It is not essential, but outward posture often reflects inward attitude and may help contribute to it.

11. Turn anything you found helpful in your reading into prayer . . . of praise or petition.

12. Some have found the letters ACTS helpful: A = Adoration, C = Confession, T = Thanksgiving, S = Supplication.

13. Rejoice when such times feel as if they are periods of re-vitalisation.

14. Press on, even when they don't — the Quiet Time blesses you, even when you don't realise it.

QUESTION

The word 'World' and 'Worldly' seems to have various connotations in Christian's minds and indeed in the New Testament. I should welcome any help you can give.

ANSWER

The main word translated 'world' is kosmos. It refers to an arrangement or order, usually of mankind. There are three ways in which 'world' may be used. The first is the physical earth, for which another word (oikoumen) is usually used. The second is society. When Jesus told the disciples to go into all the world to preach the gospel, it is used in this sense. The third sense is more sinister, that of society in rebellion against God. Thus John states 'the whole world lies in the power of the wicked one' (1 John 5 v 19). Jesus prays for His disciples not that they should be taken out of the world, but that they shall be kept from the evil in the world (John 17 v.15). A monastic existence finds no warrant in scripture.

This balance is beautifully illustrated in the life of Jesus. He is described as 'our high priest, holy undefiled,' separate from sinners and they it. A Christian's deep friendships must not be among ungodly men who do not know the Saviour — 'bad companions ruin good character' (1 Corinthians 5 v 33). We must not let the world squeeze us into its mould, as Phillips' paraphrase of Romans 12 v 1 & 2 so strikingly puts it. The way we can avoid this is by allowing a greater influence to take hold of our lives — the Holy Spirit is to re-mould our lives from within.

The word (or worldliness) which is harmful to the Christian is summarised in 1 John 2 v 15, 16 'Love not the world, neither the things that are in the world. If any man love the world, the love of the Father is not in him. For all that is in the world, the lust of the flesh, and the lust of the eyes, and the pride of life is not of the Father, but is of the world.' In considering whether conduct is worldly, here are some good questions to pose:

1. Does it glorify God?

2. Does it promote my Christian life or endanger it?

3. Does it help or hinder my weaker brother?

4. Does it promote my witness or hinder it?

5. Does it please the Holy Spirit or grieve Him?

6. Does it lead me into God's will or out of it?

7. Does it adorn the doctrine?

I like the definition of Oliver Cromwell, writing to his daughter, 'Worldliness is anything which cooleth thy desires after Christ'.

QUESTION

When considering 'Christian Lifestyle', what kind of areas should we think about apart from possessions?

ANSWER

This is what a good deal of the New Testament is all about! The epistles usually commence with great doctrinal truths and then apply them to practical Christian living. The epistle to the Ephesians is a good example. Its opening chapters deal with the wealth of the believer — the glorious riches we have in Christ. It then proceeds them to our work.

1. We should walk worthy (Ephesians 4 v 1). This deals with our relationship to fellow-Christians. We are to make every effort to maintain this unity of the Spirit through the bond of peace. To achieve this be completely humble, and gentle, be patient, bearing with one another in love (v 2). Humility is not a strange feeling inside, but when I abase myself for the blessing of others.

2. We should walk differently (Ephesians 4 v 17). We will not win the world by becoming like the world, but by becoming like Christ. We should shun the standards and practices of a permissive society.

3. We should walk affectionately in love (Ephesians 5 v 2). This means a life poured out for the blessing of others, just as Christ loved us and gave Himself for us.

4. We should walk purely in light (Ephesians 5 v 2). We should avoid unclean actions. 'There must not be even a hint of sexual immorality or any kind of impurity' (5 v 2). We shall avoid unclean talk. 'Nor should there be any obscenity, foolish talk or coarse joking, which are

out of place, but rather thanksgiving' (5 v 4). It is worth remembering also that of some things done in darkness it is a shame even to speak (5 v 12). If we plumbed the depths of sin prior to conversion, that does not mean that all the lurid details have to be recounted in a testimony. Rather, a veil should be drawn over that which God has forgiven and forgotten. That advice applies to writing also. Sensationalism may sell literature, but it doesn't minister to spiritual well-being.

5. We should walk circumspectly — in line (Ephesians 5 v 15). We shouldn't fritter away our time, 'making the most of every opportunity because the days are evil'. We shouldn't get 'drunk on wine, which leads to debauchery' (5 v 8). That means not participating in the boozy do at the office. Instead, we should be filled with the Holy Spirit.

QUESTION

How much importance would you attach to experience in the Christian life?

ANSWER

One of the most penetrating statements of Jesus on this subject was 'You do greatly err not knowing the scriptures nor the power of God.' There is a cold orthodoxy which is utterly correct in its doctrinal stand but which is sterile. The i's are dotted and the t's are crossed, but there is no vibrant inner life. It is of interest that great movements of God's Spirit in England in a bygone day, stemming from different theological origins — i.e. the Puritan Revival and the Weslyan Movement, both laid great stress on the inner life of a believer and his communion with God.

Conversely there is the other error of those who stress experience to the exclusion of the scriptures and this is perhaps the greater cause of confusion today. The error is equally bad. A young man came to see me. He was a Christian but going out with a girl who was not. I counselled him that this was wrong, because the Bible made it plain. His answer was 'But I feel led to go out with her.' I had to reply that wherever his leading came from, I did not know, but it was certain it did not come from God, who was not self-contradictory. The scriptures are still the final authority in all matters of faith and conduct, and all our views and experiences must be brought to this touchstone.

QUESTION

Why does sanctification take such a long time?

ANSWER

That is rather like saying 'Why does growing up take such a long time?' Because it is the nature of things, would be the obvious answer. In one sense sanctification is instantaneous. 'Jesus Christ is made unto us sanctification', and again in 1 Cor. 6 v 11 says 'you are sanctified'. As far as God is concerned we have been set apart for holy use, which is what sanctified means. That is our standing in Christ. But to be conformed to His likeness requires a lot of work! A lifetime's work, to be precise, and at the end of it there'd be a radical re-shape needed. But again, for each situation we can know instantaneous holiness within the limits of our knowledge. The power is available through Christ, and then victory can be ours (the athlete should always have the potential to win the race, if he has kept in training so that the intrinsic power can be released). Yet it is only within the limits of knowledge, since the closer we come to the light the more cleanliness is revealed, which is doubtless why the levitical law prescribes sacrifices for deliberate violations and for unrealised sins.

QUESTION

We see from the Bible that in the early church miracles were an everyday occurrence. Jesus is the same yesterday, today and forever. He loves the early church and the disciples as much as he loves people today. God shows no favouritism, all men are equal.

Why then are miracles a rare occasion? Or perhaps something that just missionaries talk about? Surely miracles should be the 'norm' in our everyday experience with the Lord, just as in biblical times?

ANSWER

Miracles occurred in 'outbreaks' in the Bible — particularly in the times of Moses, of Elijah and Elisha and of Jesus and the early church. They were not continuous throughout the Old Testament, nor have they been continuous in the church's history. On each occasion they were to vindicate the authority of servants of God. With the completion of the canon of scripture, miracles on the scale of apostolic days died out.

Having observed these facts of history, it is worth emphasising that miracles are with us today. Every time someone is born again that is a miracle. Moreover, it is a greater miracle than a physical manifestation, in that it is of eternal significance. This is doubtless what Jesus meant when he said, 'greater works than these shall you do'. In the proclamation of the gospel worldwide we are privileged to see miracles of grace greater in extent than during the ministry of Jesus, since His immediate impact was confined to Israel. It would also be a mistake to imagine that a succession of dramatic miracles would bring people to faith in Christ. In the wilderness the children of Israel experienced 40 years of miracles. They produced a generation of sceptics, none of whom (with two notable exceptions) entered the promised land.

QUESTION

When I pray, I picture Jesus from a painting. Now I wonder if I have made it an idol. If it is wrong, what should I do?

ANSWER

The commandment is crystal clear. We are not to make any graven images. This is doubly so in the light of the New Testament where we are taught to walk by faith not by sight. It is interesting how a good thing can be turned into an idolatrous object when used for worship. The brazen serpent used to cure the people after they sinned in the wilderness, later became a focus of idolatry as it was venerated by the people (you may see a striking parallel with the crucifix).

We know virtually nothing of the physical features of the Lord Jesus, save that He had no beauty that we should desire Him — and His face was marred more than that of any man. His *wounds* are the features on which the Bible majors.

For these reasons I am reticent about using pictures of Christ, even in children's books, Nor do I like to see Him portrayed in drama. How an actor with artistic sensitivity could ever have the arrogance to think he could enter into the character of Christ is quite beyond me. For all that, we do need to form pictures in our mind — the human mind is a picture gallery, not a library, a point preachers would do well to remember. The important thing is that Christ should be central to our thinking, and any picture that comes unbidden into our mind secondary. Equally important, we should pray whether a picture is formed or not.

QUESTION

Why do Christians seem to lose their enthusiasm as they get into the late 20s and 30s, and what is the best way to prevent this happening?

ANSWER

This is all too common. Young people who were on fire in their Christian Unions sink into an easy-going church life. The reasons are outlined in the parable of the wedding feast when invited guests made excuses — I have bought a field I must go and see it; I have bought some oxen and must try them; I have married a wife. These reasons keep men from Christ, and dampen their spiritual enthusiasm.

1. The World. As people become prosperous they forget God. The children of Israel were warned about this before entering the promised land. In the parable of the sower Jesus said that the deceitfulness of riches, the cares of this world, and the lust of things were the thorns which choked spiritual vitality and made men unfruitful.

2. Work. The demands of busy and absorbing careers dull the cutting edge of many Christian testimonies. We forget the Lord's injunction, 'Seek first the kingdom of God and His righteousness, and all these things will be added unto you.' Be careful that when you think you are finding your place in the world, it isn't the world that is finding its place in you.

3. Weddings. The comfort, security and responsibilities of home life take their toll. Happy is the man that has a wife who spurs him on to greater efforts. It is in an important criterion a young man should seek in choosing a life partner.

Here are some tips on how to prevent it:

1. To be forewarned is to be forearmed. Think carefully about the Biblical principles above.

2. Live an all-out, sacrificial, soulwinning life from your early Christian days.

3. Be careful of teaching that suggests you are too busy. It is more likely that you are insufficiently disciplined. The devil rarely tempts anyone to hard work.

4. Maintain your discipline of regular prayer and Bible reading. I am appalled by the number of Christians of some years standing who have never read the Bible through.

5. Be a regular prayer meeting goer. Wherever you find yourself make this a priority — and pray when you get there.

6. Keep involved in lively evangelistic work.

7. Stir up your soul by reading good Christian biography — not frothy sensationalism, but the lives of men and women who were sold out for God and lived consistent, sacrificial lives (if you can obtain the series published by the Moody Press, do so) — Hudson Taylor, C. T. Studd, Boreham of Yale, Adoniram Judson, Henry Martyn, David Brainerd.

8. Don't be discouraged by hard graft. The test is not the speed of short bursts. but endurance in the marathon.

QUESTION

A lot of older Christians as they grow older slow down. How can I prevent that?

ANSWER

Regrettably this is true, and many older Christians seem to be like Asa who in his old age was diseased in his feet. The first thing is to recognise the dangers. Remember that the cares of this world and the deceitfulness of riches are likely to choke your spiritual vitality. A man who goes to war does not entangle himself with the affairs of this world, and it will be a healthy preventative step not to become too involved with matters of this world. Many of us in courting days would do outlandish things to meet and to talk with out best beloved. Should we do any less for the Lord than we would do for self? It is well to keep this thought before us. Keep deeply involved with a vigorously evangelising fellowship. Moreover, if you have the choice of two paths, choose the hardest. The devil rarely baits his traps with hard work.

QUESTION

If we are not under law but under grace are there any things which we must do as Christians?

ANSWER

First of all we must understand clearly what we mean by being 'under grace'. The theme is expounded in Galatians, where it is made clear that our salvation is utterly and entirely dependent on what God has done in Christ, and it is in no way supplemented by our works. This is one of the errors of Roman Catholicism where salvation is by faith and works. New Testament teaching is that Salvation is by faith alone. However, that faith which is alone is not saving faith. A saving faith automatically issues in good works, and if good works are absent then the professed faith is dead (James 2 v 17).

So, we are saved by faith alone. Nevertheless, the Gospels and Epistles contain clear injunctions to holy living. The moral law of the Old Testament in the Ten Commandments is expanded in the New Testament, so that thoughts and intents are deemed as bad as actions. We now keep that law however, not in order to save us, but because we are saved. And the indwelling power of Christ by the Holy Spirit is available to enable us to do. We work out our salvation in the fear and trembling because it is God who works in us to will and to do of His good pleasure.

Our motives too are different. We endeavour to keep the law (moral precepts) not out of a sense of legalistic obligation, but because the love of Christ constrains us (2 Cor. 5 v 14). We find that love is the fulfilling of the law (ie it fills in the loopholes, Romans 13 v 10) — you can usually find a way around the letter of the law, but constrained by love divine you have a very different attitude in which you follow the spirit of the law well beyond the letter. 'If you love me,' said Jesus, 'keep my commandments' (John 15 v 14).

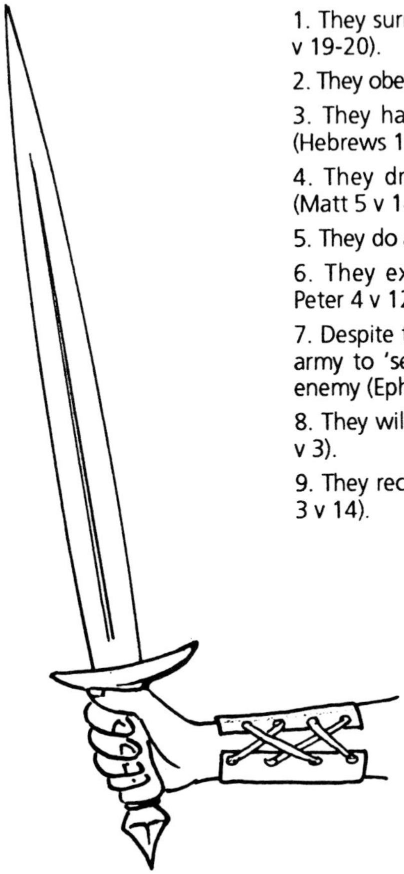

QUESTION

What does it mean to be a soldier of Christ?

ANSWER

The metaphor is a good one. Just think of ordinary soldiers, and consider how we should be with Christ, the captain of our salvation (Hebrews 2 v 10).

1. They surrender their own will (1 Cor. 6 v 19-20).

2. They obey marching orders (Phil. 2 v 12).

3. They have their friends behind them (Hebrews 11 v 24-26).

4. They draw attention as they march (Matt 5 v 14-16).

5. They do as they are told (John 15 v 14).

6. They expect to meet difficulties (1 Peter 4 v 12-16).

7. Despite the posters, they are not in the army to 'see the world' but to fight the enemy (Eph. 6 v 12).

8. They will ensure hardship (2 Timothy 2 v 3).

9. They receive rewards for valour (1 Cor. 3 v 14).

QUESTION

What do you think of the present 'Health and Prosperity teaching' as being the right of all believers?

ANSWER

The error of this teaching lies largely in a failure to appreciate that the emphasis of the gospel dispensation is that the children of God are a *spiritual* people not a physical people. Many of God's promises were given to certain people for a certain time. Moses stretched his rod over the Red Sea and it parted. I would be likely to have a watery grave if I did the same.

'But,' replies someone, 'isn't Christ the same yesterday, today and for ever?' *He is unchanging in His person, but not His purpose.* As the children of Israel marched through the wilderness their clothes never wore out, their footwear never required repair, their food was provided miraculously every day, and none of the diseases afflicted them. Those promises and provisions were for that period.

In the purposes of Christ we are permitted to suffer. Indeed, from earliest days the church has been a suffering church. Paul had a permanent illness, which wasn't cured despite insistent prayer. Others were left behind sick in his missionary journeys. The church has been tortured on the rack of pagan and papal Rome. Some of the greatest saints have suffered incredibly. John Bunyan was imprisoned for 13 years for his Christian testimony — all the time tearing his heart out for his blind daughter who sold matches to provide comforts for her beleaguered father. Young lives have been snuffed out as pioneer missionaries. God has something better than physical guarantees. These sufferings work for us as a far more eternal weight of glory. The suggestion that the suffering saints down the ages to the present have not enjoyed God's best is a slur on the Saviour. We must never forget that we are the bride of Christ, that He loves His bride, and that His dealings with us are always for the best.

QUESTION

How does a person know that they have been called by God to preach? What Scriptural principles are there to guide this person?

ANSWER

We are called to preach, whether it be one to one, or to a crowd. I presume you mean in a 'fulltime' capacity, so that you are chargeable to a church — a solemn step since it costs two people's salaries (the one you are paid and the one you would earn in ordinary employment).

Things I would ask are:

1. Do you have a burden to do it?

2. Do you speak in the open air? Charles Haddon Spurgeon used to be strong on this point — if you haven't taken these opportunities freely available to you the likelihood of a call to the more restricted indoor ministry is small (cf Lectures to My Students).

3. Do you receive numerous invitations to preach?

4. Are others aware of your ability in this respect? — Point (3) partially answers this, but you should consult others, particularly the elders of your church.

5. Ultimately, the decision is one you must prayerfully make before you and the Lord.

6. Do maintain a flexibility of approach. Because you have been to a Bible College doesn't mean you have to go into 'full-time' work. It certainly doesn't mean you are a second class citizen if you don't. Nor does it mean that if you are 'fulltime' at one stage of your life, the Lord expects that will always be so. If Paul could take up the role of a tentmaker, we must be prepared to do the same.

QUESTION

How can God use us as tools for the salvation of others?

ANSWER

1. We need to be clean instruments. 'If any one purifies himself from what is ignoble, then he will be a vessel for noble use, consecrated and ready for any good work ' (2 Timothy 2 v 21). Notice that it says any *good* work, not any *great* work. Many of us seek a great work, whilst we should be prepared to be involved in good work.

2. We should be concerned. The Master soulwinner was 'moved with compassion'. We seldom hear these days of a passion for souls — more is the pity. We desperately need it.

3. We should be prayerful. If Jesus said concerning the demon possessed boy, 'This kind comes not out except by prayer and fasting', we may be sure that the greater work of a soul's salvation will not be accomplished at less cost. Personally, and at the church prayer meeting, we will be pleading for souls.

4. We should be up and doing. The promise of reaping is to those who go forth and sow (Psalm 126 v 6). You don't win if you don't enter the race. You are not promoted if you don't start the job. The world's adage is that if a thing is worth doing it is worth doing well. Should that consideration stop you doing things on the grounds of being ill-prepared, remember that if a thing is worth doing, it is worth doing badly. You may have to learn on the job!

5. Grasp the principles of Psalm 123:1-2, 'I will lift up my eyes to you, to you whose throne is in heaven. As the eyes of slaves look to the hand of their master, as

the eyes of a maid look to the hand of her mistress, so our eyes look at the Lord our God, till He shows us His mercy'. We are small vessels in the hand of a great God. We look to the Lord in submission and obedience, knowing that the blessing will follow.

QUESTION

How would you witness to a non-Christian family?

ANSWER

'Let your light so shine before men that they see your good works and glorify your Father which is in heaven.' Holiness begins at home; sanctification begins at the sink. Live in such a way that mother exlaims, 'Whatever has come over our Susan; she gets up early, makes her own bed, leaves the room tidy, washes the dishes and doesn't answer back any more.' That will really back up the words of testimony you give.

Avoid confrontation situations wherever possible and try to share with your parents still — indeed more so than before. If father is keen for you to go to the seaside on Sundays, ask mother how you are going to solve the problem, since you'd like to go to church, although you would love to go with them other times.

At all times honour your father and mother. At times you may not be able to admire them (e.g. father may be an alcoholic), but never reject them. Always consider them to be important people. That means you'll pray for them daily, and seek to take them along to hear the gospel as the opportunity arises.

Bring your Christian friends home — but keep the bad examples away.

QUESTION

How do you answer a man who says he is an atheist?

ANSWER

You could always say, 'That makes two of you.' Inevitably he will ask, 'Who is the other?' You can then point out that the Bible says, 'Then fool has said in his heart there is no God.' It is a polite way of telling him he is a fool.

Overwhelming evidence for the existence of God is to be found in *creation*. 'What may be known about God is plain . . . because God has made it plain. For since the creation of God's invisible qualities — His eternal power and divine nature — have been clearly seen, being understood from what has been made, so that men are without excuse' (Romans 1 v 19,20).

Such evidence is also to be found in the Bible. The only rational explanation of the wonders of the Bible (especially fulfilled prophecy) is that it was inspired by God. The culminating evidence is in the person of Christ. His sinless life, His saving death, and His startling resurrection can only be explained on the fact that He was the eternal Son of God.

QUESTION

What do you say to the atheist who sees Christianity and religion as a way of ignoring reality . . . a laugh?

ANSWER

1. Distinguish carefully between Christianity and other religions. Many religions are ignoring reality (escapism). The phrase 'Religion is the opiate of the people' was first coined not by Karl Marx but by Charles Kingsley, an Anglican clergyman. Kingsley (author of 'The Water Babies') was only too well aware that formal religion solved nothing and could be disastrous in that it lulled men into a sense of false security.

2. True Christianity is not escapism, although it offers a way of escape which is most needful.

3. Your friend needs to face the realities of life — that God exists and has revealed Himself — that we are sinful (which is only too apparent to your conduct and to our conscience) — and that we are going to die.

4. Your friend may choose to ignore these facts. 'There are none so blind as those that will not see.' Remember that Cain became a practical atheist before he became a philosopical atheist. In that case you must continue to pray earnestly for him, to live in such a way that your life commends the risen Saviour, and to invite him to hear the gospel from time to time whatever rebuffs you get. People may grow up to more sensible positions, circumstances do make people aware of their need, and prayer changes things.

QUESTION

In these days of permissiveness what counsel would you give to parents with young families? Many things that were absolute when many of us were youngsters now seem to have been compromised and the violation of them has become the norm.

Nobody would advocate a return to the old time sabbaths, with children of tender years having to endure perhaps three sessions of church attendance, but Sunday has now, for children and parents alike, become a mere extension of Saturday as a day for trips to the seaside etc. with Sunday School attendance in the summer months sadly depleted.

What has happened to the respect and deference children were once obliged to show to parents and school teachers, and what of discipline? The Bible teaches, both Old and New Testaments that children should be trained and punished, old fashioned as that may sound in the ears of today's free expression kiddies.

As a Christian parent yourself, I feel that some advice from you on this very real problem will be of great value to many sincere young parents who are seeking to train up their children in the love and nurture of the Lord.

ANSWER

1. Establish in the home an environment of love and security.

2. Teach Biblical truths. This was a powerful factor in the way Timothy came to the Lord, 'From a child you have known the holy scriptures, which are able to make you wise unto salvation through faith which is in Christ Jesus' (2 Timothy 3 v 15). It was a keystone in bringing up the family of Old Testament days. 'Never forget these commands. Teach them to your children. Repeat them when you are at home and when you are away; when you are resting and when you are working' (Deut. 6 v 6, 7).

3. Maintain Christian standards:

(a) in terms of honesty.

(b) in terms of purity (watch the television—or better still don't watch it).

(c) in terms of respect for authority—within the home, at school, and elsewhere in the community.

(d) in terms of concern for others — the natural cruélty of children needs to be checked and a care for the less fortunate inculcated.

(e) in terms of the Lord's day—those who lose respect for the Lord's day soon lose reverence for the Lord of the day.

(f) in terms of church attendance —parents who only go once a Sunday need hardly be surprised if their children come to think that meeting with the Lord's people is of little moment, and services are to be endured rather than to be enjoyed.

4. Recognise that discipline is not a dirty word, but essential for producing a responsible citizen, let alone a man of God. The precepts of the Bible are clear, 'Discipline your children while they are young enough to learn. If you don't you are helping them to destroy themselves, (Proverbs 19 v 18).

The examples of the Bible are equally clear. Eli was a godly priest, but failure to correct his sons Hophni and Phineas brought reproach on God's name and wrested the privilege of the priesthood from Eli's family. David's softness with his son Absolom provoked a rebellion.

The best comment on present day permissiveness which despises discipline was the answer given to the modern mother who avowed that all her child needed was a pat on the back, 'Yes, ma'am, as long as it is low enough and hard enough'. A spoiled brat is a burden to his parents, an embarrassment to visitors, a potential menace to society, and basically an unhappy child. To have fair, firm guidelines is an important factor in establishing security. Coming down the mountain trail on the side of a precipice is a much more enjoyable experience when there are protecting rails to warn and help the unwary.

6. Pray daily: pray earnestly; pray together for their spiritual welfare.

The questioner kindly enclosed with his query the prayer of commitment from the Festival of Light International Year of the Child rally at All Souls, Langham Place. Here is part of it:

> FORGIVE US, and forgive this nation, for our neglect of our children, through ignorance, through weakness and our own deliberate fault.
>
> We have given them material things and forgotten spiritual truth:
> We have given them freedom and forgotten discpline:
> We have spoiled them often, but failed to love them;
> We have done much for our children, but little for the disadvantaged children of others . . .
>
> the unborn — the poor, — the handicapped — the homeless.
>
> We have neglected our family life, and the care we should have given to the wounded and broken families of our nation.
>
> LORD GOD, whose Son came on earth as a child into a human family, FORGIVE US through the blood of Jesus Christ, Our Saviour and Lord.

QUESTION

How do we help people to really grow as a Christian? Why do some people never seem to grow no matter what they hear?

ANSWER

If you like alliteration, it is through food, fresh air, friendship and fitness — just like a natural child.

1. *Food.* The Bible clearly teaches that as newborn babies we should desire the sincere milk of the Word. The Bible before breakfast was Job's motto,and it should be ours — he put it 'your word have I desired more than my necessary food.'

2. *Fresh air.* 'Prayer is the Christian's native breath'. We need to set time aside to seek the Lord.

3. *Friendship.* Inter-personal relationships are just as important in spiritual growth as they are in natural development. Isolationism has no part in Christian culture. It is together that we grow and glow.

4. *Fitness.* Exercise develops bonny babies and healthy adults. Get stuck into Christian work. Remember that the best way to learn is to teach.

Some people never grow because they have never been born. If a person shows no signs of growth, you should check carefully whether they have ever truly become a Christian. Certainly they have no reason to have an assurance of salvation. Moreover, to hear is not enough. All food and no exercise produces obesity not growth. They may need to be galvanised into action.

QUESTION

How would you witness and handle serious back-sliders? I know some who say they are 'Bored' with the gospel

---

ANSWER

First, you make a diagnosis. Is the person truly a Christian? From your question — I doubt if they are. If someone is 'bored with the gospel', I doubt their salvation. A Christian loves the gospel:

'Those who know it best
Seem hungering and thirsting
To hear it like the rest.'

No person walking in deliberate sin can have any certainty of salvation. A desire for holiness is an important plank in the platform of assurance. Enquire carefully about the circumstances of their professed conversion. Explain carefully the gospel, woo them for Christ, and warn them of the consequences of rejecting Him.

If you think the person is a Christian, try to identify the sin which took them away from Christ. It may be a wrong relationship (don't be unequally yoked with the unbeliever), wrong friends (bad company corrupts good morals), wrong activity (sin will keep you from the Bible, as surely as the Bible will keep you from sin), or wrong attitudes, eg. those who desire to be rich fall into temptation and a snare, and into many foolish and harmful lusts which drown men in destruction and perdition. 'For the love of money is a root of all kinds of evil, for which some have strayed from the faith in their greediness, and pierced themselves through with many sorrows' (1 Timothy 6 v 9,10).

People often suggest that slackness in the quiet time is a cause of backsliding. My experience is that this is a symptom rather than a cause. Proverbs 14 v 14 states, 'The backslider in heart will be filled with his own ways.' Self has to be dealt with. Point out to the backslider how wrong may be rectified. Plead with them to return to our loving Saviour, who is as willing to receive and restore them as Hosea was to buy back a faithless, enslaved wife. Pray earnestly for this restoration. Live before them as one who is crucified with Christ, so that it is evident that the life you now live is by the power of our indwelling, risen Christ — and trust that His life manifest through you will draw them.

QUESTION

What can you say to friends who say that they want to give up their faith?

ANSWER

Firstly you must make an accurate diagnosis, and then prescribe the remedy. It may be that the person has never come to saving faith. Their so called faith may have been based on inadequate knowledge. When Paul asked the Ephesians 'Have you received the Holy Ghost since you believed?' (Acts 19 v 2), their faith was based on a defective gospel. It may be that your friend has been following Jesus as a great teacher, but never seen Him as the Saviour who gave His life as substitute for our sins.

Again, your friend may appreciate these truths intellectually but never fled alone to Jesus for refuge. This of course was the mistake John Wesley made as an Anglican clergyman. He knew the facts of the Gospel, but had never committed himself to the Lord Jesus Christ, as the One who alone could save him from his sin, absolutely and entirely independent of his good works.

If, however, your friend appears to have committed his life truly to Christ and given evidence of the new birth (Acts 2 v 42), further investigation is required. The fire goes out if you don't refuel it, or if you let the ashes clog it up. There may be concealed sin. Demas forsook the faith because he loved this present world (2 Timothy 4 v 9). Your faith will either separate you from the world, or the world will separate you from your faith.

The love of money and desire for material possessions will cause people to err from the faith (1 Timothy 6 v 10).'But thou, O man of God flee these things; and follow after righteousness, godiness, faith, love, patience, meekness. Fight the good fight of faith' (1 Tim. 5 v 11,12).

A wrong relationship commonly draws away from the faith (clear examples are Samson and Solomon).

Sitting beneath unsound ministry that makes little of Jesus and His redeeming work, and undermines the authority of God's Word, the Bible, will have a deadening effect.. Since faith comes via the Word of God, any belittling of it will weaken faith. The strategy of the devil in Eden was first to cast doubts on God's Word and then on God's character before he introduced the temptation that brought about the banishment of our fore-parents. Doctrine does matter. Shun vain and profane babblings.

QUESTION

What comfort can you give to someone who has lost a loved one who lived and died without acknowledging a faith in God?

ANSWER

This is one of the most difficult situations and must be approached with the greatest tact and sympathy. The major thoughts which frame my help to such a person are:

1. We never know what goes on in the heart and mind of a person in the closing moments. Transactions can be wrought within even when a person cannot speak.

2. 'Shall not the judge of all the earth do right?'. We can rely utterly on God who is just and merciful.

3. Weep with those who weep. We may not be able to give definite assurances but a sharing of sorrow can help to lift the burden.

4. Job's comforters were the maximum help when they just sat silently with him. The troubles began when they insisted on talking!

5. Jesus understands our sorrows. There are just some indications that His father (Joseph) died when He was young, so that He knew family bereavement. Certainly we know from the episode at the grave of Lazarus that He enters into human suffering at such times.

QUESTION

What do you say to a person who says 'I've tried it and it doesn't work?'.

ANSWER

Jesus spoke of those who 'tried it' without any lasting results. In the parable of the sower, some seeds fell on shallow soil. Initially it looked very promising, but because there was no depth it quickly withered under the scorching sun of opposition. Other seed did even better, but it was choked by the cares of this world, the deceitfulness of riches, the lust of things.

First therefore, you must ascertain the category into which the person fits. You do not tell them they did become a Christian. A 'decision' and being 'born again' may not be the same thing to all. It may be they have never appreciated the dreadfulness of sin and the need to turn away from it. 2 Timothy 2 v 19 is an important statement in this context, 'Nevertheless, God's solid foundation stands firm, sealed with his inscription: "The Lord knows those who are His"' and 'Everyone who confesses the name of the Lord must turn away from wickedness'.

It may be that they have never appreciated the heart of the gospel 'that Jesus Christ died for our sins, according to the scriptures'. Jesus Christ came to be a substitute for sin not a substitute for satisfaction — hence the inadequacy of teaching which merely urges people to 'get turned on to Jesus' or 'to come to Christ for real kicks'. The person may not have appreciated that the basis on which we enter Christian experience is 'to flee alone to Jesus for refuge'. It is not a matter of 'having the guts to stand up for Jesus' — the emphasis must always be on what He has done for me, and my casting myself upon His mercy. The person may not have appreciated that Christ has a rightful claim to be the Lord of our lives and this is essential to the gospel. 'If you confess with your mouth 'Jesus is Lord', and believe in your heart that God raised Him from the dead, you will be saved' (Romans 10 v 9).

INDEX

INDEX